How to Shape Your
Kids Better

Hari Datt Sharma

Published by

F-2/16, Ansari Road, Daryaganj, New Delhi-110002
☏ 011-23240026, 011-23240027 • *Fax* 011-23240028
Email info@vspublishers.com • *Website* www.vspublishers.com

Regional Office Hyderabad
5-1-707/1, Brij Bhawan (Beside Central Bank of India Lane)
Bank Street, Koti, Hyderabad - 500 095
☏ 040-24737290
E-mail vspublishershyd@gmail.com

Branch Office Mumbai
Godown # 34 at The Model Co-Operative Housing, Society Ltd.,
"Sahakar Niwas", Ground Floor, Next to Sobo Central, Mumbai - 400 034
☏ 022-23510736
E-mail vspublishersmum@gmail.com

Follow us on

All books available at **www.vspublishers.com**

© Copyright: 𝒱&𝒮 PUBLISHERS
ISBN 978-93-813842-6-8
Edition 2014

The Copyright of this book, as well as all matter contained herein (including illustrations) rests with the Publisher. No person shall copy the name of the book, its title design, matter and illustrations in any form and in any language, totally or partially or in any form. Anybody doing so shall face legal action and will be responsible for damages.

Printed at Param Offseters Okhla New Delhi-110020

Preface

Raising well-balanced children is an art. The sincerity of parents in discharging their responsibility towards their children will reflect in the development of the latter. In other words, as parents sow, so shall they reap – in the form of well-balanced or maladjusted children. Proper upbringing demands active effort, concern, sensitivity, skills, understanding and empathy on the part of parents. Children are always dependent on their caretakers to look after their physical, mental and emotional needs. Which is why, a child is a reflection of the parents' behaviour.

It is impossible to write a perfect prescription to mould ourselves into caring and successful parents. However, there are some guidelines that parents may find quite useful. One must note that there are many variations in parents, as there are in children. Furthermore, when we talk of parents and couples, we are not dealing only with two people but also with the net result of their interaction with each other. Also, remember that there are some prerequisites for effective parenting, just as there are for most tasks.

Every child needs emotionally stable parents who are mature and love each other. In homes where there is only one parent, his/her task becomes very complex, as s/he must take on many additional tasks ordinarily handled by the other parent.

Parents need to demonstrate their love for their children not only by their actions but also by the kind of environment they create in their homes. A child develops a feeling of security and confidence when he knows that he is loved.

Parents need to develop some understanding of their child's personality, as his talents, interests and aspirations mature. With this understanding, they can assist the child in aiming more accurately towards his goals, thus helping him fulfil his objectives.

Through discipline, guidance and encouragement, parents provide opportunities for the healthy exploration of natural surroundings by the child. They foster curiosity in their children to help them realise their full potential. Children who are deprived of such opportunities tend to fear the unknown and the future.

Parents must encourage children to express their true feelings. Successful parents imbue their family with a sense of belonging and provide opportunities for democratic planning and social action.

Consideration of and help for individual and family problems must be provided readily. The test of the genuineness of a problem lies more with the intensity of feeling about it, than with the nature of the problem itself. There are times when the father's needs must be, at least temporarily, relegated to second place because of the needs of his child. Successful parents constantly seek better ways to do what they have to do without affecting their attention towards their children.

A child's maladjustment with society often results from a poor parent-child relationship, which in turn often stems from lack of correct understanding by parents about their children. An adverse upbringing and the contemporary family situation are two powerful factors of maladjustment. Symptoms of emotional upheaval in a child point towards a disturbed parent-child relationship. When the child realises that being naughty is the only way to attract attention, he indulges in naughtiness.

Emotional problems in children do reflect through their misbehaviour like fighting, lying, stealing, destroying property or breaking rules.

These traits constitute the *acting out behaviour*. This is the misbehaviour that a child indulges in to express his emotional turmoil. In other words, this misbehaviour is an outward expression of a child's emotional disturbance. Through it, he signals his emotional insecurity, hostility towards parents and feelings of inferiority. For example, lying results from the child's attempt to secure attention and gain esteem. Children who lie also consistently try to overcome insecurity through chronic stealing. Their attempts at stealing openly and getting caught in the process show their hostility towards parents. In some cases, the stolen items symbolise parental love, power or authority, which the child feels deprived of.

Depressive reactions and other emotional problems in childhood are often masked. Among young children, irritability, temper tantrums, low tolerance, hyperactivity and sleep disturbances are common reflections of depression. Among older children, disobedience, running away from home and delinquent behaviour may mask an underlying depression.

Masking of emotional problems is not restricted to children only. In adolescents too, depression may commonly be masked by their inability to sleep, gastrointestinal upsets and chronic fatigue.

This book provides useful tips to parents to help their children develop normally – physically, mentally, emotionally and academically. Ignorance by parents about their child's special emotional and other needs can spoil the whole life of a child.

The main purpose of this book is to provide you with the necessary information to make you successful parents. Morals are imbibed and not taught. As the parents sow, so shall their children reap.

—Hari Datt Sharma
Founder
Peace of Mind Mission
New Delhi

**Ten Commandments for a
Child's Behaviour Development**

1. *When children live with encouragement, they develop CONFIDENCE.*
2. *When children live with tolerance, they learn to be PATIENT.*
3. *When children live with criticism, they learn to CONDEMN.*
4. *When children live with ridicule, they learn to be SHY.*
5. *When children live with hostility, they learn to FIGHT.*
6. *When children live with praise, they learn to APPRECIATE.*
7. *When children live with shame, they learn to feel GUILTY.*
8. *When children live with security, they learn to have FAITH.*
9. *When children live with approval, they learn to LIKE themselves.*
10. *When children live with acceptance, they learn to find LOVE.*

Contents

Preface 3

1. **Parental Behaviour that Plays Havoc with Children** 9
   - Overprotection and Restrictiveness 10
   - Rejection – a Masked Deprivation 11
   - Over-permissiveness and Indulgence 12
   - Parental Over-expectations 13
   - Faulty Discipline 14
   - Favouritism......................15
   - Maternal Deprivation.....16
   - Faulty Family Patterns ...16
   - Failure in Communication............18
   - Early Psychic Trauma 19
   - Ten Commandments for the Child's Behaviour Development 19

2. **As Parents Sow, So the Children Reap** 21
   - Family Circumstances Abetting Maladjustment...............21

3. **Childhood Behaviour Disorders** 25
   - Stuttering (Stammering) 25
   - Bed-Wetting (Enuresis)...28
   - Sleep-Walking (Somnambulism)............30
   - Research Findings...........31
   - Problem Sleep..................32
   - Excessive Sleep.................33
   - Unrealistic Fears...............33
   - Phobic Neurosis 35
   - Temper Tantrums............36
   - Hyperactivity...................38
   - Anger Spasm and Breath-Holding..............40
   - Tics (Habit Spasm)..........41
   - Shyness & Withdrawal...42
   - Stealing 44
   - Lying.....................................45
   - Thumb Sucking 45
   - Rocking and Head Banging..........................47
   - Hair Plucking...................48
   - Mud Eating 49
   - Nail-Biting.......................50
   - Runaway Reaction..........51
   - Voluntary Silence 52
   - Faecal Soiling (Encopresis)....................53
   - Attention-Seeking Devices.............................54
   - School Phobia 56
   - Gifted Children 57
   - What Makes Some Children Aggressive? ...58
   - Typical Case Histories....60

4. **Ways to Improve Children** 62
   - Behaviour Modification Techniques 62
   - Play and Family Therapy 63
   - The Importance of Token Economies 64
   - The Child's Emotional Growth..............................64
   - The Importance of Motor Development 66
   - Teaching Social and Personal Skills.................68

- Role of Punishment 70
- Fostering Creativity 72

5. **Influence of the Environment on Children............................74**
   - Impact of Divorce on Children..........................74
   - Influence of the Employed Mother.........75
   - Sibling's Influence............76
   - Why Children like Comics 76
   - Goal-directed Behaviour 78
   - Infant's Emotions.............79
   - Crying..................................79
   - Smiling................................80
   - Laughter 80
   - Effect of TV on Children's Behaviour....80
   - Findings of UNESCO Study 82
   - Adjustive Mechanisms to Release Tension..........83

6. **Helping Children Develop Basic Skills 85**
   - Methods of Learning 85
   - A Developmental Schedule 86
   - Main Development Norms 87
   - Common Words in Children's Books 90
   - Developing Skills in Written Communication 93
   - Handwriting 93
   - Spelling..............................94
   - Written Expression..........94
   - Main Reading Skills........94
   - Readiness for Arithmetic 95
   - Auditory (Phonic) Readiness........................96

- Auditory Sequential Memory 96
- Readiness for Learning 96
- Reading Readiness..........97
- Basic Skills Required 97
- Checklist For Parents......98
- Assessing the Child's Reading Readiness..........98
- A. Mental Maturity 99
- B. Background of Experience.....................100
- C. Social Readiness 101
- D. Emotional Readiness.......................102
- E. Specific Abilities........102
- Visual Readiness 102
- Visual Retention 103
- Visual Discrimination...103
- Auditory Readiness......104
- Motor Readiness 105
- General Notes.................105
- Vineland Social Maturity Scale............106

7. **How to Treat Common Learning Difficulties.....110**
   - Common Learning Difficulties and Methods of Treatment.................110

8. **Caring for Handicapped Children............................113**
   - Crippling and Health Disabilities.................... 113
   - Hearing Disabilities......115
   - Visual Disabilities 117
   - Mental Retardation 117
   - Handicapped Children Need Special Education 117
   - Typical Adaptive Behaviour Expectancies 119

1

Parental Behaviour that Plays Havoc with Children

Contemporary research findings in the biological and social sciences have greatly advanced our understanding of the causes of abnormal behaviour exhibited by humans. It is mainly due to faulty development, severe stress or a combination of both.

When any child imbibes criminal values, he may become a criminal due to his faulty development. Faulty development is primarily responsible for the signs of abnormal behaviour in humans. The type of adjustment we are able to develop with people around us at any time is a function of both our personality development and the level of stress we face. Anything that leads to either faulty development or increased stress may create trouble.

If an individual is able to cope effectively with stressful situations, anxiety is eliminated. But if the anxiety and stress continue, the individual typically resorts to various ego-defence mechanisms, such as denial and rationalisation. This may result in lowered integration and maladaptive behaviour. The process of self-defence leads to incongruence between reality and the individual's competence. One should always bear in mind that *faulty learning is the main cause of faulty behaviour*.

Let us now understand the Ten Evils that play havoc with children.

Evil No. 1

Overprotection and Restrictiveness

Excessive maternal protection is called *momism*. It involves smothering the child's growth. Overprotective mothers watch over their children constantly, protect them from the slightest risk, and overly clothe and medicate them. They take decisions on their child's behalf at every opportunity, not allowing them to think for themselves. Different parental motivations may lead to overprotection.

Overprotection can decrease the urge to explore and take risks. And to the overprotected children, other children and adults may seem like awesome, frightful figures.

When the child's desire to seek independence are thwarted, he becomes frustrated. This sows the seeds of aggression and hostility in the child-parent relationship.

The mother's anxiety about the world is readily transmitted to the child. This provides a fertile ground for phobias, as well as for physical illness, which may be unconsciously encouraged by the mother if she has hidden motives to keep the child at home with her.

Overprotection may also cause excessive shyness and, as adults, these children might not be able to express themselves properly and be unable to take decisions independently. Ultimately, it may result in the following symptoms: temper tantrums, anger spasms, failure in school, school phobia and the like. All these end up in imparting an inadequate personality to the child. Such children often reach adolescence and early adulthood feeling inadequate and threatened by a "dangerous" world.

Closely related to overprotectiveness is restrictiveness. Here the parents rigidly enforce restrictive rules and standards, giving the child little freedom for growing in his own way.

In a study, Becker (1964) concluded that while restrictiveness fosters well-controlled socialised behaviour, it also tends to nurture fear, dependency, submission, repressed hostility and some dulling of intellectual striving. Often, extreme behaviour on the part of an adolescent is a way of rebelling against severe restrictions.

Main Causes of Overprotection
1. When a boy is born after a succession of girls in a family.
2. When s/he is the only child.
3. When the death of a sibling occurs.
4. When the child is handicapped.
5. When the child happens to be adopted.
6. When the child is born after the parents are past their prime.
7. When there have been a series of miscarriages.
8. When either of the parents is no more.

Evil No. 2
Rejection – a Masked Deprivation

Parental rejection of the child, though unintentional, is shown in various ways. This could include physical neglect, denial of love and affection, lack of interest in the child's activities and achievements, harsh or inconsistent punishment, failure to spend time with the child, remaining busy in activities like kitty-parties and lack of respect for the child's rights and feelings as a person. It could also involve cruel and abusive treatment. Parental rejection may be partial or complete, passive or active, and subtle or overtly cruel. Keeping the child in a crèche can also be a form of rejection.

The effects of rejection manifest in the child in the form of excessive fear, shyness, aggressiveness, thumb-sucking, bed-wetting, depression, temper tantrums, lying, stealing, slow morality development, low self-esteem, a feeling of insecurity, loneliness and an inability to express and receive love. All these arise at the subconscious level and the child cannot prevent their manifestation in his behaviour or personality.

Parental rejection is a major reason why adolescents run away from home.

Causes of Rejection

It appears that a large number of parents who neglect their children have themselves been victims of parental rejection. Later, even children who face parental rejection don't accept their parents when the latter grow old. So, rejection is not a one-way behaviour. That is why lack of love has been referred to as a *communicable disease*.

A child may be neglected without being rejected. For instance, when parents are too busy with their work or career, they neglect children.

Evil No. 3
Over-permissiveness and Indulgence

Allowing too much freedom of behaviour to children is called *permissiveness*. And allowing a child to do or have whatever s/he wants is termed *indulgence*.

Sometimes one or both parents seem always ready to indulge their child's smallest whims. In doing so, they fail to inculcate a desirable standard of behaviour in him. When parents indulge their child too much, it is bad for the child's development.

Overindulged children are characteristically spoiled, selfish, inconsiderate and demanding.

It is found that high permissiveness and low

punishment at home are positively correlated with *anti-social and aggressive behaviour*, particularly during the middle and later childhood.

Rejected and emotionally deprived children often find it difficult to enter into warm interpersonal relationships. When indulged children do enter into such relationships, they try to exploit people for their own interests in the same way that they have learned to exploit their parents.

If made to yield to authority, such children often turn rebellious, since they have had their own way for long.

Overindulged children also tend to be impatient. They approach problems in an aggressive and demanding manner. They find it difficult to accept present frustrations in the interests of long-term goals. The fact that their important and pampered status at home does not hold true in the outside world comes as a rude shock for indulged children. Confusion and difficulties in adjustment may occur, when reality forces them to reassess their assumptions about themselves and the world.

Evil No. 4

Parental Over-expectations

Some parents place excessive pressure on their children to make them live up to unrealistically high standards. Such parents expect their wards to excel in school and other activities. In the case of children who have the capacity to perform exceptionally well, things may work out to the parents' satisfaction.

Even so, the child may be under such sustained pressure that little room is left for spontaneity or development as an independent person. Mainly, the child is unable to quite live up to parental expectations and demands. If he improves his grade from C to B, he may be asked why he did not get A. Even if he succeeds in getting the A grade, the next expectation is to get an A+!

The parents always tell the child that he could do even better if he works harder. But no matter how hard he tries, he seems to fail in the eyes of his parents and, ultimately, in his own eyes. This results in painful frustration and self-devaluation. As the child is unable to live up to his parents' high expectations, his efforts seldom get parental approval and appreciation. This tends to discourage the child from making more efforts. The child eventually feels – I can't do it anyway, so why try?

There is nothing wrong with parental expectation vis-à-vis children. They help the child aim for a goal, which is good for his development. But expectations and demands that are too high (or too low) or distorted and rigid, can be a major cause of the child's faulty development and maladjustment.

Evil No. 5
Faulty Discipline

Many parents still believe that if they spare the rod, they will spoil the child. This indicates that many parents lack general guidelines for the proper upbringing of their child. One day, they may punish the child, but the very next day, they ignore his follies or even reward him.

Over-permissiveness and lack of discipline tends to produce a spoiled, inconsiderate, aggressive child. On the other hand, harsh discipline may have a variety of harmful effects, including fear of and hatred for the punishing person, curbing of initiative or spontaneity and less friendly feelings towards others.

Combined with restrictiveness, severe discipline also tends to incite rebellion and socially deviant behaviour in children, as they grow older.

When the child commits some folly, if the parents resort to physical punishment instead of withdrawal of approval and privileges, it may result in an increase in aggressive behaviour. Similarly, inconsistent discipline makes it difficult for the child to imbibe stable values to guide his behaviour.

When the child is punished once but ignored or rewarded the next time for the same behaviour, he is at a loss to understand what behaviour is appropriate. Parents must realise this and make it clear to the child too, that *it is the child's behaviour that is disapproved of and not the child itself*. The child must know clearly what kind of behaviour is expected from him, and to make this happen, positive and consistent methods of discipline should be worked out.

Evil No. 6

Favouritism

This arises from a variety of causes, which are more or less similar to those resulting in overprotection. The main causes: **1.** If the child is better looking or more intelligent than the other sibling. **2.** If there has been a sequence of girls and, finally, the much-desired boy is born.

The favoured child will encounter the same problems described earlier for the overprotected child. On the other hand, the disfavoured child may feel resentment against the parents and, perhaps, even towards the favoured child, showing little affection for them.

Evil No. 7
Maternal Deprivation

When infants are deprived of maternal stimulation as a result of separation from the mother, e.g. she could be a working woman or due to lack of adequate mothering at home, faulty development is the natural outcome.

When the mother devotes little attention to the child and, in the process, neglects or rejects it, the effects of such masked deprivation may be devastating. Mothers who reject or punish infants may cause tense, cranky and negative behaviour even at that early age. In case of early and prolonged deprivation, the damage to the infant may be irreversible or only partially reversible. Mothers who are regularly away at kitty-parties or inflict separation on their infants due to other preoccupations, and those who keep their child in a crèche, should be careful.

Evil No. 8
Faulty Family Patterns

As the infant grows into childhood, he must master new skills, learn proper assumptions about himself and the world and exert inner control over his behaviour. During this period, the family unit remains the crucial guiding influence for the child's personality development. Faulty family patterns are a fertile source for unhealthy development and maladjustment.

Recent research has revealed that maladjustive behaviour shown by the child may be fostered by the general family environment, as well as by the child's relationship with one or both parents.

An inadequate family lacks the resources, physical or psychological, for meeting demands with which most families can satisfactorily cope. The inadequate family relies heavily on sustained outside assistance and support in resolving its problems. Such a situation may stem from immaturity, lack of education, mental retardation or other shortcomings of the parents. Such families cannot give their children the feeling of safety and security they need, or adequately guide them in the development of essential competencies.

A disturbed family atmosphere has a bad effect on the child

In some disturbed families, parents are always fighting to maintain their own equilibrium and are unable to give the child the much needed love and guidance. Parental conflict and general tension are unfortunate conditions for the growing child.

Children tend to observe and imitate the behaviour of their parents. The parents prove to be undesirable role models for the children when they go by faulty realities, possibilities and value assumptions. It has a bad effect on the child if the parents depend excessively on defence mechanism in dealing with their problems. Examples of defensive behaviour: they blame one another or others for their own mistakes, they lie and cheat, they refuse to face and deal realistically with family problems and there is a marked discrepancy between their proclaimed values and those reflected in their actual behaviour.

A parent who is emotionally disturbed, addicted to alcohol or drugs, or otherwise maladjusted serves as an undesirable role model for his child.

In some families, parents engage in behaviour that violates the norms and interests of society. Children in such families simply observe and imitate the undesirable behaviour and attitudes of their parents. They may also acquire negative behavioural traits, like dishonesty, deceit, etc.

Maladaptive behaviour is much higher among children and adolescents from disruptive homes. Disruptive families are incomplete, whether as a result of death, divorce, separation or some other circumstances. Divorce leads to feelings of insecurity, rejection and conflicting loyalties. The loss of the father is more traumatic for a son than for a daughter.

Undesirable parental models are an important cause why mental disorders, delinquency, crimes and other forms of maladaptive behaviour tend to run in families.

Evil No. 9
Failure in Communication

Parents who discourage their child from asking questions fail to foster in him the skill that is essential for healthy development of his personality. Some parents are too busy with their own concerns to listen to their children. Consequently, they are unable to understand the conflicts and pressures their offspring are facing. During a crisis, such parents often fail to give the desired support and assistance to their children.

Many parents may convey one message by their words and another through their behaviour. For example, a father may deplore lying and sermonise to his son, "Never tell a lie", while he himself is prone to lying at the slightest pretext!

It is also a damaging communication pattern when parents, due to any prejudice or misconception, contradict or undermine the child's statements and conclusions, and he is left confused and devalued as a person.

Evil No. 10
Early Psychic Trauma

Many people have had traumatic experiences that temporarily shattered their feelings of security, adequacy and worth. Such experiences later on play a major role in influencing their evaluation of themselves and the environment they live in. These traumas are bound to leave psychological wounds that never heal completely. That is why, one person feels quite stressed while facing a particular problem, while this is not at all stressful for the other person.

Early traumas seem to have more far-reaching consequences than later ones, because critical evaluation, reflection and self-defences are not yet well developed in children.

Ten Commandments for the Child's Behaviour Development

1. When children receive regular encouragement, they develop *confidence*.
2. When children are taught tolerance, they learn to be *patient*.
3. When children are exposed to criticism, they learn to *condemn*.

4. When children live amidst ridicule, they learn to be *shy*.
5. When children live amidst hostility, they learn to *fight*.
6. When children receive praise, they learn to *appreciate*.
7. When children live with shame, they learn to feel *guilty*.
8. When children live in security, they learn to have *faith*.
9. When children live with approval, they learn to *like* themselves.
10. When children live with acceptance, they learn to find *love*.

ooo

2

As Parents Sow, So the Children Reap

Family Circumstances Abetting Maladjustment

Within the family circle emotions run wild and deep. The home is in many ways a miniature world, for here are found the forces that shape personality, the feelings that will determine the quality and quantity of relationships a child will form with his peer group and, ultimately, with his intimate adult companions.

While it is true that during the school years the child becomes less homebound, nonetheless the influence of parents during this period is profound. The home establishes rules, ideas and values by which the child comes to measure life and those who share his life.

Given below is a brief description of the families where children are prone to acquire negative behavioural traits:

1. **Antisocial Families:** In these families, parents are overtly or covertly engaged in behaviour that violates the norms and interests of society. Children in such families may be taught or may themselves emulate acts of dishonesty, deceit and other undesirable behaviours and attitudes of their parents.
2. **Disturbed Families:** In disturbed families, children are prone to psychological disorders. Here, parents with grossly eccentric and

abnormal personalities may keep the home in constant emotional turmoil.

3. **Inadequate Families:** Such families are unable to cope with ordinary problems of family living due to lack of resources. These families cannot give their children the required feeling of safety and security. Also, they cannot adequately guide and encourage their children to develop skills that are essential to succeed in life.

4. **Disrupted Families:** These families come into being as a result of the death of a parent, due to divorce or separation or some other circumstances. Children of these families suffer from insecurity and rejection complex.

5. **Mother Threatens to Desert:** In some families, the mother often threatens to desert or sometimes actually deserts the family for short periods. In such families, the child is likely to show mother-anxiety symptoms. Often, the child will develop hostility towards the mother.

6. **Deep Estrangement Between Parents:** In a family where deep estrangement prevails between parents, the mother attempts to satisfy her thwarted need for affection by overindulging her son, especially the eldest one. She uses him as a means of annoying her husband. Consequently, violent antagonism develops between father and son, with the son openly blaming the father for the family troubles. The critical point is reached when the mother loses her nerve under severe strain and turns on the boy, accusing him of being the source of trouble.

7. **Mentally Ill Mother:** In a family where the mother is mentally ill and her mental disturbances have reached a stage where the strain of living

with her has become almost unbearable, the father will try his best to be away from home. He will find other sources of part-time recreation that will make his presence at home much shorter.

8. **Lack of Maternal Concern:** The mother's lack of concern for the child often results in the latter being left with the grandmother or some other woman. In such a scenario, the child will develop and express affection for the foster mother or its father.

9. **Father's Long Absence From Home:** When the father remains away from home due to some reason during the child's early years, it seems a form of emotional rejection for the child. This causes a disturbance in the child, which the father interprets as bad behaviour. He fears that other children will become affected with his child's crankiness. This attitude often causes quarrels between the parents, which may result in the mother herself turning against the child for the sake of "family unity".

    Threats to have the child put away in a hostel-like institution produce a counter-reaction of self-banishing hostility. The child resorts to creating a nuisance, running away and stealing within the home. Often, this situation is caused by the anxious-hostile personality of the father, but it can also arise in families of highly principled parents who take too serious a view of the child's lying and other misdemeanours.

10. **Mother Forced to Bear Undue Strain:** In some cases, the father exerts undue and excessive pressure on the mother, through sickness or an inability to work, through unbalanced behaviour

or by lack of support in running the family. Consequently, the mother faces a combination of mental stress, sheer physical overwork and an inability to manage her family, thereby reaching a stage of irritable, depressive non-tolerance. In this state, she reacts violently against any source of disturbance or annoyance. She may even temporarily express dislike for her child.

11. **Child's Preference for Grandmother:** In some homes, the child shows his preference for the grandmother rather than his mother. Because the grandmother shields the child from the mother's disciplinary nature, she is regarded as the epitome of kindness and all good things, while the child rejects the mother as she is the one who denies, disciplines and punishes. But later on, in the absence of the grandmother or another motherly figure, the child cannot easily reverse this attitude towards his real mother. In such a situation, unable to exercise any discipline, the real mother may allow herself to be dictated to by the child in a bid to regain her child's affection.

12. **Child Fearing Abandonment:** In some cases, the child fears he will be abandoned. This fear of abandonment may be due to adoption, remarrying of the mother after a divorce or death of the father. In such instances, the fear of abandonment may induce in the child an inhibition against any affectionate attachment and he may develop violent hostility.

ooo

3

Childhood Behaviour Disorders

STUTTERING (STAMMERING)

Stuttering is a speech disorder characterised by blocking of sound or a struggle to speak, resulting in a repetition of words or sounds. The speaking pattern of the stutterer may vary from mild difficulty with initial syllables of certain words to violent contortions and momentary inability to utter any sound at all. Many stutterers can speak fluently under normal circumstances, but they tend to stammer during moments of important or stressful communication.

Stuttering is more frequent in boys, with barely 20% of victims being girls. The peak onset occurs before the age of six in about 90% of cases, with the highest incidence occurring between two and four years of age. A stutterer also exhibits a few motor behaviours, like eye blinking, jerking of hands, tremor of the lips, frowning, swallowing, fist clenching, feet stamping and the like.

Most victims experience no difficulty when they sing, whisper, count, recite memorised poems, believing that they are alone and unobserved or while speaking in a dark room. Sometimes, they also speak other languages fluently. This speech disorder represents an internal struggle to speak. After the initial disturbance, the speech may become smooth and fluent, until the next stumbling block. The difficulty may vary considerably from one situation to another.

Stuttering increases both in severity and frequency in situations where the stutterer feels inferior, self-conscious or anxious.

Some researchers have suggested there are four different types of stutter: emotional, nervous, respiratory and habitual.

Causes

It appears that stuttering could develop from various stressors that hamper normal speech, particularly during the early stages of speech development.

Any stressful situation that leads to severe feelings of inadequacy, self-consciousness, anxiety, fear and tension also tends to impair psychomotor co-ordination and performance. This may include speech functions. Why stressful situations affect speech functions more in some persons than others is not known. However, stuttering is largely a psychological problem, despite notions to the contrary.

This speech disorder greatly affects the personality of the stutterer. Once the child becomes aware of his abnormal speech patterns, he tends to reduce the frequency of speaking and may even go into hiding when guests visit the home. Stuttering results in high levels of shyness and sensitiveness.

Treatment

Stuttering is treated through speech therapy and various other methods that could include aversion conditioning, desensitisation, rhythm exercises, assertiveness training, hypnosis, social reinforcement of fluency and the delay of auditory feedback.

These methods are generally divided into two categories.

The first category's methods focus on direct elimination of stuttering. The methods in the second category involve a two-step treatment: *acceptance* and then *elimination*. For example, methods such as Demosthenes speaking with pebbles in the mouth, aversion conditioning and the delay of auditory feedback fall into the first category. Here the attempt is to achieve fluency by means of some special techniques with the hope that this fluency carries over into the individual's normal life.

The second category's treatment is based on the view that the stutterer does not want to face stressful situations. The conflict tends to produce a vicious circle in which the impending fear increases the likelihood of stuttering. *The first step here is for the stutterer to accept the reality that he is a person who stutters, but can be cured of this.*

The second step focuses on achieving speech fluency in now-successful situations in which the individual formerly stuttered. Desensitisation, self-assertion, reinforcement and other therapy approaches may be applied here. Once fluency is achieved, the vicious circle is broken and positive feedback and reinforcement tend to maintain the fluent speech pattern.

With appropriate treatment, most stutterers can be completely relieved of their symptoms or be greatly helped. However, a method that proves quite effective with one stutterer may be ineffective with another. Therefore, a stutterer may need to try different treatments to see what works for him.

For getting better results from any form of therapy, it is absolutely necessary for parents to create an environment in which there is minimum anxiety, tension and disapproval. They should make the child realise that they approve of his speech regardless of how he speaks. A friendly relationship should be developed between the parents and the child. The child should not be criticised or ridiculed. Parents must listen patiently to the child for what he has to say rather than the way he says it.

Here is a brief outline of some stuttering therapies:

Assertion Training: This is a behaviour therapy procedure that attempts to help a person more easily express his thoughts, wishes and beliefs, including feelings of resentment or approval.

Aversive Conditioning: Here, harmful stimuli are used to punish unwanted behaviour. However, this is not a method that is generally recommended and in some cases could exacerbate the problem, rather than improve it.

Desensitisation: This is a therapeutic process by which reaction to traumatic experiences are reduced in intensity by repeatedly exposing the individual to them in mild form, either in reality or through fantasy.

BED-WETTING (ENURESIS)

In medical parlance, bed-wetting is called *enuresis* and refers to the habitual involuntary discharge of urine after the age of three. It is more common at night but it may also occur during the day.

Among older children, enuresis often occurs in conjunction with dreams in which the child imagines that he is urinating in a toilet. He immediately wakes up to discover that he has wet the bed.

Enuresis commonly occurs from two to five times a week.

Causes

Enuresis may result from a variety of organic conditions. But most researchers attribute bed-wetting to the following causes:

a) Faulty learning or lack of toilet training. This often results from maternal over-protection and the mother's lack of knowledge about proper

toilet training. The result is a failure to acquire the necessary adaptive response, that is, inhibition of reflex bladder emptying.
b) Personal immaturity associated with or stemming from emotional problems.
c) Disturbed family atmosphere that leads to sustained anxiety and hostility.
d) In some instances, a child may regress to bed-wetting when a new baby is born in the family and replaces him as the centre of attention.
e) The child may resort to bed-wetting when he feels hostile toward the parents and wants to get even with them.
f) It is also regarded as a revenge responsive case, which is in retaliation to the nagging, punitive attitude of the mother.

Treatment

The main difficulty facing enuretic children is that they have not learnt to wake up before bed-wetting occurs. This is because the body mechanism (i.e., bladder tension) does not arouse them from sleep.

In western countries, special electrified mattresses are used on children's beds that ring an alarm on receiving the first few drops of urine, thus waking the child and eliciting a reflex stoppage of micturition. These mattresses have proved successful in the treatment of bed-wetting.

Bladder control during daytime should be taught to the child by the middle of the second year. The child should be made to sit in the toilet at specific hours, e.g., after waking up and before and after meals. The child should not be taken to the toilet frequently and his toilet stay should not exceed more than a few minutes.

Scolding, punishing or mocking the child is not the

answer for his failure to control the bladder. The child should not be awakened at night if he is less than two years old.

A different learning treatment for enuresis is based on the theory that enuretics have an abnormally small functional bladder capacity. Some experts suggest that the child should be asked to perform exercises to gradually increase the volume of urine that he can retain before emptying the contents of his bladder.

Some experts suggest not giving any liquids to the child at least two hours before he goes to bed. The child should be trained to pass urine before he goes to sleep.

Sometimes bed-wetting is also found to be associated with urinary tract infection, worm infestation and the like. These causes should be treated with the help of a doctor or child specialist.

SLEEP-WALKING (SOMNAMBULISM)

Some children experience regular or periodic sleep-walking episodes. These children usually go to sleep in a normal manner, but get up during the second or third hour of their sleep and carry out some act.

This sleepwalk may take the child to another room of the house or even outside and may involve rather complex activities. Such episodes usually last from 15 minutes to about an hour. The child finally returns to bed, but in the morning he cannot recall anything that had taken place during his sleep-walk. During sleep-walking the child's eyes are partially or fully open, he avoids obstacles, hears when spoken to and ordinarily responds to commands, such as being told to return to bed.

Shaking a sleep-walking child will usually awaken

him and he will be surprised and perplexed to find himself at an unexpected place.

Causes

The causes of sleep-walking are not fully understood. It has been found that sleep-walking takes place during the non-rapid eye movement phase of sleep. Hence it does not represent the acting out of a dream, as is commonly believed.

In general, it would appear that sleep-walking is related to some anxiety-arousing situation that has just occurred or is expected to occur in the near future.

Treatment

Psychotherapy – the treatment of mental disorders by psychological methods – is considered useful in sleep-walking. It primarily consists of verbal means of helping troubled individuals change their thoughts, feelings and behaviour in order to reduce distress and achieve greater life satisfaction.

Research Findings

Recordings of brain waves, eye movement and other parameters have shown that there are four stages of sleep, progressing from light sleep phase to deep sleep phase.

According to research findings, a normal adult spends about 20 percent of his sleep in Stage 1. This is considered the main stage for dreaming, in which Rapid Eye Movement (REM) occurs. Of the remaining sleep duration, about 60 percent occurs in immediate stages 2 and 3, and about 20 percent in the deep sleep of stage 4. Although some dreaming may also occur in the latter stages, they are referred to as non-REM or NREM sleep. The individual goes through all these four stages in 90-minute cycles from light through deep sleep and back again to light sleep.

Although we do not understand the precise role of REM and deep sleep in maintaining normal physiological and psychological functioning, it appears probable that disturbed sleep patterns in depression, schizophrenia and other mental disorders play an important interactive role.

PROBLEM SLEEP

Generally, the overanxious and withdrawal reactions of childhood appear to result in sleep disturbances, oversensitivity, unrealistic fears, nightmares etc.

Failure to sleep when parents expect them to may be due to the unrealistic expectations of parents.

In the first four weeks after birth, most babies wake up twice for feeds in the night. By about ten weeks, the night feed is dropped but the babies may still get up due to some disturbance. At the age of about six months, children may awaken with a sudden scream due to a nightmare. Between the ages of two and three years, children may awake due to a full bladder.

Causes

Insufficient and restless sleep may result from bodily discomfort produced by wetness, tightness of nappy, hunger, thirst, cold, or excessive heat. It may also occur due to pain in the abdomen, blocked nose, itching, eczema etc.

In older children, it may be due to emotional immaturity, excessive strain of work, fear of examinations, maternal separation, etc. Nightmares may also disrupt sleep. Nightmares are common in healthy children.

Treatment

No formal treatment is required. Make sure that the child is sleeping in a comfortable position wearing comfortable clothes. Open-air exercises in the evening may help in initiating sound sleep.

EXCESSIVE SLEEP

Many children spend a great deal of daytime in sleep but it doesn't reduce even a minute from their night sleep. This type of excessive sleep may be caused by the following reasons: lack of interest in school and homework, both the parents being out because of their service, monotonous home environment with no facilities for entertainment, or due to some physical illness.

UNREALISTIC FEARS

Most of us harbour various kinds of fears. All normal children also have fears. Fears constitute a normal defence mechanism. But it is harmful when fear is exaggerated and starts causing anxiety. Children often develop fear of darkness, ghosts, strangers, animals, vehicles, fire, water, death, and even fear of desertion by parents, fear of death of the father, mother, brother or sister etc. Young children acquire such fears from their immediate surroundings and respond to them by undifferentiated behaviour.

Children fear loud noises, frightening gestures, scary tales, nightmares, deformities, bad people, robbers, supernatural events and bodily injury. Children also fear being scolded, embarrassed, teased and ridiculed.

Causes

The causes of childhood fears and worries are closely related to the development level of the child. Many fears arise from the ignorance of the environment and the child's inability to cope with them.

Fear responses have a tendency to become generalised. For example, a specific situation generates fear in a child. Later, when the child comes across a new situation containing some elements of the previous fear-provoking situation, he immediately responds with a fear reaction.

School-going children encounter many unknown and strange circumstances and more or less constantly live in a fear-producing environment. They are so accustomed to the general emotional state of fear or worry that they anticipate the condition. In other words, they worry when there is nothing to worry about.

A child may also acquire fears from his fearful overprotective mothers. For instance, the mother's own fears of spiders, thunderstorms, or men hiding in the shadows in the street at night may also make her child fearful about such things. Single frightening experiences may lead to the developing of a phobia, and consistent avoidance of the feared situation means that the fear is never tested in reality and given the chance to be extinguished. Some fears may be developed in the child by the foolish threats of parents who attempt to force the child to eat, sleep or pass stool.

Children's fears often affect them physically and they suffer from headaches, stomach-ache and nausea, and they also vomit sometimes.

Treatment

As children grow older, they are eager to understand their environment.

Increasing use of their intellectual abilities enables them to discover many facts for themselves. Fear by itself is undesirable, but fear that matures through knowledge and critical evaluation is desirable. That is, it is a good idea to look before you leap. A mature person is able to distinguish between fear justified by knowledge and experience, and fear based on ignorance.

Fear can be eradicated by the removal of insecurity caused by overprotection, domination etc. The child should be made more familiar with the objects or situations he fears. If he is afraid of water, he should be encouraged to play with water. Treatment based on behaviour therapy is most effective.

Exposure is generally agreed to be the most effective way of eliminating fear and avoidance of something that does not merit caution. Modelling has also proved effective; the fearful child is likely to demonstrate fearless behaviour when rewarded for moving closer to a feared object or situation. This can encourage the child to venture forth.

Phobic Neurosis

A phobia is a persistent fear of some object(s) or situation(s) that present no actual danger to the person. In a phobia, the perceived danger is highly magnified compared to its actual seriousness.

The following list of some common phobias and their objects gives some hint of the variety of situations and events around which phobias may be centred.

Acrophobia: fear of heights or high places

Agoraphobia: fear of open places

Algophobia: fear of pain

Astraphobia: fear of storms, thunder and lightning

Claustrophobia: fear of closed places

Haematophobia: fear of blood

Mysophobia: fear of contamination or germs

Monophobia: fear of being alone
Nycrophobia: fear of crowds
Pathophobia: fear of disease
Pyrophobia: fear of fire
Syphilophobia: fear of syphilis
Zoophobia: fear of animals or some particular animal.

TEMPER TANTRUMS

Childhood depressive reactions and other emotional problems are often masked among young children. For example, irritability, temper tantrums, intolerance, hyperactivity and sleep disturbances are common reflections of depression among older children. These children act out their frustration through disobedience, running away from home and through delinquent behaviour. All these characteristics may create an underlying depression.

Outburst of bad temper in a child is called a *temper tantrum*. Anger and frustration are the basic cause of temper tantrums. All children are constantly subjected to many frustrating experiences. It is thrice as common in boys than in girls. For example, on a father's refusal to buy his son a costly toy, the latter starts pulling his clothes, tearing the books kept in a shelf, beating his younger brother, etc.

When any child throws a tantrum, he often screams, stamps his feet, kicks, strikes people, curses, thrashes his arms around, throws himself on the floor, bangs his head, bites and throws things around.

An outburst of bad temper

Causes

Tantrums are more common up to the age of five, after which there is a progressive decline with age. Tantrums may be precipitated by a variety of situations, basically the same ones that produce feelings of anger in adults. This problem usually occurs in an active, energetic and determined child due to the clash of the child's developing personality with the will of the parents.

The child wants to show his power, to gain attention and to practise new skills and to take responsibility for doing things that he has recently learnt.

When the child encounters parental resistance in achieving his objectives, he throws tantrums. His tantrums are further aggravated when the parents talk to friends about his dreadful behaviour in his presence.

If badly managed, a single tantrum is likely to develop into a habit, as the child has discovered a satisfying way of annoying his parents.

Overprotection and overindulgence increases indiscipline in children, thus aggravating their tantrums. Through temper tantrums, the child sometimes also wants to show his resentment against any unwelcome situation, such as visiting the doctor or going to any place he doesn't like.

If the mother permits a child to do a particular thing but the father forbids this, it may lead to a temper tantrum and the ultimate erosion of parental authority.

Treatment

First of all, the faulty attitude of parents in the form of overprotection, overindulgence and over-strictness and the consequent insecurity felt by the child will have to be remedied. The opportunities for parental resistance must be cut down to a minimum. The child should be kept occupied. He should have playmates of his own age in the house. He should also be allowed to go out to visit playmates in their homes.

The child should be encouraged to practise skills and to take pride in what he can do. *His tantrums should be ignored. He should not be given what he wants after a tantrum.*

The child will stop throwing tantrums as soon as he finds that he will get nothing after doing so.

HYPERACTIVITY

A common childhood disorder, hyperactivity is characterised by over-activity, restlessness and distractibility. It occurs with the greatest frequency before the age of eight and tends to become less frequent and of shorter duration thereafter. It disappears by the mid-teens.

Hyperactive children suffer from a disease called *Hyperkinetic Child Syndrome* or *Attention Deficit Disorder*.

The symptoms include short attention spans, easy distractability, impulsiveness, poor motor coordination, low frustration tolerance, emotional instability, changeable moods, hypersensitivity and lack of inhibition.

These children do not differ in intelligence from comparable groups of normal children. However, they do tend to talk continuously and could be socially uninhibited and immature. Usually, they do poorly in school, commonly showing specific learning disabilities such as difficulty in learning to read or in learning other basic school subjects.

Here is an example of such a girl. In the words of a counsellor: "Kamla was a hyperactive girl. She was a problem for her teacher and to other students because of her hyperactivity and uninhibited behaviour. She would impulsively hit other children, knock things off their desks, erase material on the blackboard, damage books and other school property. She seemed to be in perpetual motion – talking, moving about and darting from one area of the classroom to another. From parents and teachers, she demanded an inordinate amount of attention, and was intensely jealous of other children, including her own brother."

Causes

The exact cause of hyperactivity is not known. There are many psychological factors that could lead to hyperactivity. For example, among hyperactive children there is a higher-than-average number of premature births. Hyperactive children are commonly assumed to be suffering from *Minimal Brain Dysfunction.*

A delay in the development of the central nervous system may be another cause. For such children, the nervous system develops more slowly but finally reaches full saturation, often at about eight to nine years of age. During the lag period, they exhibit symptoms of this syndrome.

Treatment

Even without any treatment, hyperactive reactions tend to clear up in the mid-teens. However, many children have a poor prognosis if left untreated. They show a higher-than-average incidence of delinquency and other maladaptive behaviour during adolescence and adulthood, possibly due to school failure and lack of understanding by parents.

Parents should keep valuables, breakables or other dangerous objects out of reach of such children, as they are more prone to accidents. Encouragement and recognition of achievements are essential for such children.

Cerebral stimulant drugs have a quietening effect on hyperactive children. Behaviour therapy is also useful in hyperactivity. Such children are encouraged for doing the appropriate thing, such as remaining in their seats and working on assignments. A reward is given for showing improvement. Encouragement and achievements are essential for success.

Excessive intake of beverages, tea, coffee, chocolates, food laced with preservatives, additives, artificial flavours and colouring should be avoided.

ANGER SPASM AND BREATH-HOLDING

Breath-holding spells are the most common dramatic expression of discomfort in infants and young children. It occurs any time from one to five years of age. It is more common in girls. Affected children are almost of normal intelligence.

A child starts crying when he is hurt, admonished, frustrated and frightened. In case of an anger spasm, in the midst of violent crying the child suddenly stops breathing and does not resume respiration for about half a minute. He may throw his limbs around helplessly, and sometimes his eyeballs turn upwards. This attack may last for five to ten seconds and then promptly stop.

Causes

This is a symptom of an emotional upheaval and a signal of a disturbed parent-child relationship. Anger spasm is commonly observed among children of over-solicitous parents. Experts have found that the mothers of such children are overindulgent, overprotective, over-demanding, rejecting or autocratic. It is also said that parental attitudes are the results rather than the causes.

Treatment

As the child grows up, the anger spasms start ceasing automatically and are replaced by temper tantrums or other behaviour problems. Therefore, undue or too much attention to the problem should be avoided. But if the parents suspect that their child has fallen prey to this problem, they should consult a child specialist.

However, the child should not be allowed to dominate the family with this act. Parents should exhibit an attitude of apparent unconcern.

TICS (HABIT SPASM)

A tic is a persistent, intermittent muscle twitch or spasm usually limited to a localised muscle group. The term 'tic' is used broadly to include blinking of the eyes, mouth twitching, nose picking and wrinkling, scratching, writhing hands, licking of the lips, shoulder shrugging, neck twisting, throat clearing, blowing through the nostrils, grimacing, manipulating the genitalia, thigh rubbing, pulling or twisting of hair and other responses. It may also take the form of coughing, hiccups, whistling, spitting etc.

In some instances, the individual may be aware of the tic when it occurs, but usually performs the act so habitually that he does not notice it or consider it abnormal. In fact, he may not realise he has a tic unless someone brings it to his notice.

Tics are most frequent between the age of six and 14.

Causes

Although tics may have an organic basis, most forms are psychological in origin, usually stemming from self-consciousness or tension in social situations. An individual's awareness about his suffering from tics often increases his tension in social situations because others can so easily notice it.

There is always a close correlation between intensity of movements and the severity of the emotional strain to which the patient is subjected. Tics afford the child a motor release of accumulated emotional stress.

Treatment

Tics have been successfully treated through drugs, psychotherapy and conditioning techniques.

Parents should avoid nagging or warning their child for exhibiting tics, as it may cause further aggravation. Try to improve the situation or solve difficulties due to which the tics were developed. All physical faults should receive adequate medical attention.

SHYNESS & WITHDRAWAL

A child manifesting a withdrawal reaction apparently attempts to minimise his anxiety by turning away from reality and withdrawing into himself. In other words, the child attempts to minimise his anxiety by turning inwards, detaching himself from a seemingly dangerous and hostile world. With such turning away, the child's capacity to distinguish fact from fiction tends to deteriorate. He functions inefficiently and fails to develop effective patterns of behaviour.

Such children gravitate towards seclusion, timidity and an inability to form close interpersonal relationships. They appear listless and apathetic, and are prone to daydreaming and unrealistic fantasies.

Causes

The withdrawal reaction occurs in those children who have found human contact more frustrating than rewarding. The child who is never given a chance to mix with other adults and children is likely to be shy. He may have inherited the shyness from any of his parents. Overprotectiveness by parents communicates a lack of confidence in the child's ability to cope with difficult situations, thus reinforcing his feelings of inadequacy. Repeated experiences of failure, stemming from poor learning skills, may lead to a subsequent pattern of anxiety or withdrawal in the face of threatening situations.

Treatment

Expose the child to opportunities for mixing with others and to a graded series of situations involving the actual fear-arousing stimulus. That is, separation from the mother for an increasingly longer time. The child should be allowed to invite friends to his home. He should also be allowed to go out to visit friends. Encourage the child to do things for himself.

STEALING

A certain amount of deceit seems not only common but

also apparently acceptable in society. An individual may be tempted to cheat in an examination or to be dubious in a business transaction.

Young children have a natural desire to achieve what they want. In a pre-school child, taking away things without someone's knowledge is normal development behaviour. But in a school-going child, that act will constitute stealing.

Causes

Dishonesty shown by parents at home encourages the tendency to steal in children. When the parents steal, the child may be expected to do likewise. Bad examples from peers, revenge, an antisocial personality, poverty and the like are the main causes of stealing. When parents fail to fulfil the necessary needs of the child, he begins stealing. Stealing starts at home especially from the mother and father. And once the child succeeds, he feels encouraged to repeat it again and again. Children of antisocial and poor families are the ones that mostly indulge in stealing.

Treatment

If the child steals something, he should be asked to return the same to its owner, however embarrassing and difficult the situation might be. Try to find out the causes of stealing and remove those causes. Parents should themselves desist from stealing and act as good role models for the child.

Domestic conflicts, particularly between the parent and the child, must be resolved. Take care of all the genuine needs of the child. Also keep a watch on the company he keeps.

LYING

Lying is very common in children. A child may learn the habit of lying from adults who are in the habit of exaggerating their achievements. A child may also lie to win praise, gain prestige, boost his ego, gain friends and to escape punishment from or the displeasure of parents.

Causes

Children often lie to save themselves from unpleasant situations and to avoid punishment. When parents often tell lies, children also tend to do so.

Treatment

Punishment for lying should be avoided, as it will do more harm than good. Parents should not tell lies and always avoid telling lies before children.

THUMB SUCKING

This is one of the habits of gratification. Babies have always sucked their thumbs. Though any finger or fingers may be sucked, the thumb is most frequently used for sucking.

Research shows that children develop teeth deformity if they continue thumb sucking after the age of five. Parents use all sorts of mechanical devices to make their children stop thumb sucking. Some apply ill-tasting substances on the child's fingers to make him desist from thumb sucking.

This habit is very common during the first two years of a child's life. It usually begins during the teething period. Children usually suck their thumb either constantly or shortly before going to sleep. This behaviour usually disappears at the age of five years. It is a cause for concern if it persists even after the age of three. Then it might be a sign of some hidden stress factors, which need intervention.

Thumb sucking could be a means of tension reduction

Causes

Thumb sucking typically occurs in situations associated with anxiety and/or hostility, and appears to be a means of tension reduction that provides the individual with something to do. It represents a learned maladaptive habit that is reinforced and maintained by its tension-reducing properties.

It also helps the child ward off feelings of loneliness. In times of stress, it represents withdrawal from a situation, which is too frightening to face for the child except through regression. Through thumb sucking, the infant probably relieves the pain from local irritation that may be present on his gums weeks or months before the actual eruption of teeth.

Freud regarded this behaviour as a mode of infantile sexual manifestation.

Treatment

Thumb sucking requires no treatment during infancy. Babies may be diverted from sucking the thumb by supplying them with a pacifier or rubber nipple. If thumb sucking is frequently practised after the first year of life, it means the child feels bored, over-fatigued or unhappy.

Treatment should be directed toward correcting the situation rather than focusing on the thumb sucking. The child should have sufficient rest and play. The best treatment is to divert his attention to other pleasures. If the child is pleasantly occupied with interesting activities, he will not suck his thumb.

In older children, thumb sucking should be treated through behaviour modification by promising a reward. An appeal to the child's will power or pride or to the child himself may also help. Apply any bitter tasting substance to the thumb or make him wear gloves as a reminder.

Always bear in mind that nagging or scolding will not help, but it may further aggravate the problem. The use of indigenous devices like cuffs, collars, ropes and adhesive tapes will also not help.

ROCKING AND HEAD BANGING

Some children get up on their hands and knees and rock back and forth, sometimes violently enough to hurt themselves.

In head banging, the child repeatedly strikes his head against a solid object, often the edge of the crib or against the mattress.

Rocking and banging appear when the infant is moving from one development stage to the other, i.e., from sitting to standing or from crawling to walking.

These movements are more common with the first child in the family.

Causes

It is a tension-relieving exercise as well as a means to satisfy the natural maturational needs. It may also be an attempt to gain pleasure in order to neutralise the pain of teething. It could also be related to any discomfort caused by wet nappies.

Treatment

No treatment is required. The habit ceases of its own accord. However, efforts should be made to replace these activities with more purposeful and acceptable rhythmic motor activities, such as dancing, swinging etc. In chronic cases, consult a child specialist.

HAIR PLUCKING

Some children pull their hair whenever they are tense. A few may pluck their hair, while others may eat it. In medical parlance, this is called *Trichotil Lomania*. Other forms of this problem are fingering, stroking, intensified brushing, patting, hair arranging and the like.

Causes

It is said to be an expression of conflict between the personality of the child and that of the mother or father. It is akin to an extreme degree of aggression towards oneself. Stress situations are the main cause.

Treatment

The treatment of this problem is directed at the cause. Try to find out the cause of the child's developmental struggle and the disturbed parent-child relationship, rather than focusing on the symptoms. Behaviour therapy techniques are found to be the most successful in treating this problem.

MUD EATING

Up to two years of age, children often explore the environment. They are quick to put everything into their mouth, including mud. But after this age too, some children continue to eat even non-edible substances like dust, clay, paper, clothing, wood, pencil and crayons etc.

Causes

A number of women often ignore or permit this habit because they themselves were habitual clay eaters. Mud eating may be caused due to over-protection, neglect, disharmony among parents, or the loss or separation of parents. Mental retardation, iron deficiency, anaemia, lead poisoning, worm infection, constipation and the like are also associated with this habit. In children of normal intelligence, mud eating disappears automatically.

Treatment

The most important aspect of the treatment is to find out the cause of emotional stress and to take immediate steps to attract the child to some oral substitution of the mud, such as chewing gum, food that smacks of flavour etc. In this way, the child's attention can be diverted from eating non-edible substances.

In such cases, severe threats or punishment may prove counter-productive. Instead, engage the child in play activities with games and toys. The best treatment is to alter the environment of the child.

NAIL-BITING

Nail-biting occurs in situations associated with anxiety and hostility. This habit appears to be a means of tension reduction and provides the individual with something to do when feeling tense. Some researchers suggest it is an extension of thumb sucking.

Nail-biting is usually associated with anxiety and hostility

Nail-biting is common among children but declines in frequency with age. Sometimes it persists even in adult life as a minor habit. Occasionally, the entire family is known to indulge in nail-biting. In children above three years of age, thumb sucking tends to disappear, giving way to nail-biting, which increases in incidence until the age of six. This may then continue up to 13 years of age.

Causes

Nail-biting represents a learned maladaptive habit that is reinforced and maintained by its tension-reducing properties. It provides a state of satisfaction when the child is otherwise unoccupied. It is mostly an expression of tension produced by anticipation of a difficult test in school or of parental punishment or by any kind of excitement. In broken homes and those with a tense atmosphere, the frequency of nail-biting among children is higher.

Treatment

Little attention has been devoted to the treatment of nail-biting. It is generally agreed that restraint and application of bitter-tasting substances, threats and punishments yield poor results.

Helping the child feel more adequate and secure, especially if he is going through some particularly difficult stress period, may check the initial development of this habit. The main treatment is to identify and remove the causes of tension responsible for nail-biting. Behaviour therapies like an appeal to the child, especially in the case of girls, often produce good results.

Another treatment is to keep the child busy with games and toys and healthy association with other children.

RUNAWAY REACTION

A number of boys and girls run away from home. It may occur as an isolated incident or as part of a history of *crisis flight* responses to which some young people, and even adults, resort to in highly stressful situations.

Causes

The reasons for running away from home tend to fall into three categories:
1. Getting out of a destructive family situation.
2. Running away for altruistic reasons, for example, in a desperate effort to draw attention to and change a disturbed family situation.
3. Having a secret, unshareable problem – such as a girl being pregnant or wanting a love marriage

etc.

Treatment

Family therapy is an essential part of the overall treatment programme. Parents are by no means always the primary reason for their child's running away and a "What-have-we-done-wrong" attitude may lead to unnecessary feelings of guilt.

VOLUNTARY SILENCE

Some children speak only to specific people and refuse to talk to strangers. More common in girls, this problem is generally seen in children between three and five years of age. On seeing strangers at home, they cling to their parents, whisper, hide behind furniture or cower in some corner.

Causes

This problem is caused by excessive fondness of the child for his mother. If the child undergoes a traumatic emotional experience at the time of speech development, he may develop voluntary silence. This is also a fear-reducing and attention-seeking device. Environmental factors could also be responsible for such a situation or it could be an anger-relieving device. However, at home children ask their parents endless questions about situations that worry them.

Treatment

As it is caused mainly due to stress, the stress factors have to be identified and removed. The quality of mother-child relationship has a marked effect on how the child speaks and it also determines whether the child will speak normally or not.

FAECAL SOILING (ENCOPRESIS)

This is a rare problem commonly termed as inappropriate defecation. It usually occurs when the child is awake and frequently alternates with periods of constipation. While enuresis (bed-wetting) is usually a night-time problem, soiling happens mostly during the day, very often in late afternoon. It seldom occurs at school, but often happens on the way home from school. This habit of soiling clothes decreases as age advances. Many children suffering from soiling hide their clothes.

It creates serious social problems for the child. Schoolmates avoid the unpleasant smelling child and teachers object to his presence in the classroom. Parents may become very angry and upset. The youngster himself suffers from great shame and embarrassment. He often devises clever ways of concealing soiled clothes from parents.

Causes

The main causes of faecal soiling are:
1. Separation from the mother.
2. Start of the school.
3. Over-ambitious parents.
4. Unsatisfactory relationship with the family and parents' troubled marital relationship.
5. Parental neglect.
6. Birth of a sibling.
7. Dominating and nagging mother.

Treatment

Proper toilet training should be given to the child at regular intervals to alleviate the problem. The family environment should be improved.

ATTENTION-SEEKING DEVICES

For the child, one of the paramount needs is attachment to any adult guardian. From the age of seven or eight months, there begin to appear behavioural modes that normally ensure attachment to a particular parent figure. The child expresses it in the form of smiling, appreciation of cuddling, distress at losing contact, fear of strangers following, and so on.

Children adopt many kinds of attention-seeking devices between the age of one and three. Attention seeking may take the form of bad behaviour that demands the attention of parents even at the risk of punishment. The constant demand for attention by the child from a busy or tired parent becomes a nuisance and is rebuffed by a rebuke or irritability.

Refusal to eat food could be an attention-seeking device

The main attention-seeking devices used by children are: refusal of food, screaming when put to bed, refusal to lie down, refusal to sit on the potty box, withholding of urine and faeces, the deliberate passage of stool or urine on the bed or in the room, head banging, head rolling, teeth grinding, pain in abdomen, non-interest in school work, and excessive obstinacy and the like.

Causes

In some cases, the child resorts to attention-seeking acts because his basic needs are not being recognised sufficiently as a person. Neither is he being praised and loved sufficiently nor is he being given the responsibility that he wants. When the child realises that being naughty is the only way to attract attention, he indulges in naughtiness.

Indiscriminate attention seeking by the child may also be an effect of brain damage or an outcome of anxiety about the maintenance of secure attachment.

Many children seek attention by misbehaving. Teachers and parents reward misbehaviour by calling attention to it. Children seeking attention are encouraged to indulge in that behaviour when parents and teachers quickly respond to their acts. The best way is to ignore the misbehaving child.

Treatment

The child should never be made to feel that parents enjoy his naughtiness. Most of his tricks should be ignored. Ignoring him is better than a warning or threats before the act, or punishment after the act. The child should be made to understand that he is too old for such kinds of behaviour.

The types of adjustive mechanisms that people use to relieve their tension are aggression, substitution, withdrawal, projection, suppression and reaction formation.

SCHOOL PHOBIA

This refers to a reluctance to go to school because

of an acute fear associated with it. Usually, this dread is accompanied by somatic symptoms with the gastrointestinal tract being the most commonly affected.

The somatic complaints are often used as an auxiliary device to justify staying at home, and they disappear when the child is reassured that he will not have to attend school. The characteristic school phobia symptoms are a child nauseated or complaining of abdominal pain at breakfast and desperately resisting all attempts at reassurance, reasoning, or correlation to get him to school. In its mild form, school phobia may be only a transient symptom but when it becomes established, it can be one of the most disabling disorders of childhood, in some cases lasting for years.

School phobia is not only disabling to the child and disruptive for the household, but it also appears to be a true phobia and an extreme avoidance that does not usually go away with the passage of time. Furthermore, it has serious academic and social consequences for the youngster.

Causes

School phobia is commonly thought to be rooted both in actual fear of being in school and in separation anxiety. Since the beginning of school is often the first circumstance that requires lengthy and frequent separation of the child from his parents, separation anxiety is the principal cause of school phobia.

Environmental factors that may also be related to the school setting itself elicit increased anxiety in the child. The mother may not wish to lose her child to the school each day. Fear of a teacher, threats by classmates, discrimination on the basis of caste, colour or religion, improper dress, transfer to a new class or school, and prolonged absence from school are some of the problems at school. Feeling of insecurity, birth of a sibling, hospitalisation of the mother, parental over-protection and worsening family finances may be cited as the problems at home. Mental sub-normalcy, burden of homework, anticipation of failure in exams and physical illness are several factors that prod the child in keeping himself away from school.

Treatment

Identifying and removing the precipitating factors may successfully treat this problem. Cooperative parents and teachers can jointly improve the situation.

Desensitisation is a therapeutic process by means of which reactions to traumatic experiences are reduced in intensity by repeatedly exposing the individual to them in mild form, either in reality or in fantasy.

Operant shaping is the acquisition or elimination of a response as a function of the environmental contingencies of reward and punishment.

Parents must see to it that children have the opportunity to acquire knowledge and relevant skills. For instance, a child who knows swimming will not fear water.

GIFTED CHILDREN

These are children who have *superior cognitive abilities*. Such abilities include outstanding promise or an unusual level of ability in academic attainment, creative performance, talent, the ability to deal with advanced concepts and generalisations or the generation of ideas of uncommon merit. They are endowed with creativity as well as many other talents and abilities, including high intelligence and high scholastic attainment.

Gifted children come from all ethnic, racial, social and economic groups, though in fewer numbers from the disadvantaged sections. A gifted child learns rapidly; uses lots of common sense and practical knowledge; retains what he has heard easily; knows many things that other children are unaware of; uses a large number of words easily and accurately; comprehends their meaning; recognises relations; is alert, keenly observant, and responds quickly. These children need special provision for their education.

WHAT MAKES SOME CHILDREN AGGRESSIVE?

Behaviour aimed at hurting someone or destroying something is called *aggression*. After two and half years of age, if a child kicks or punches another person, the child is showing hostile behaviour or aggression. As the child grows, this hostility may take the form of words.

Unsocialised aggressive children manifest characteristics like overt and covert hostility, disobedience, physical and verbal aggressiveness, quarrelsomeness, vengefulness and destructiveness. Lying, solitary stealing and temper tantrums are common among them. Such children tend to be sexually uninhibited and are inclined towards sexual aggressiveness. A minority may indulge in fire-setting, solitary vandalism and even homicidal acts.

Stages of Aggression
1. **Instrumental Aggression:** By age two, a child learns to get the things he wants. Aggression may take the form of snatching a toy from another child. Aggression used for securing a desired object is termed *instrumental aggression*.
2. **Social Play Aggression:** In this type of aggression, the child struggles to procure toys and control

others. This happens between the ages of three and five. As children approach the age of five and six, their expression becomes better. Now they use words. The frequency of aggression also declines. But after six years of age children become less aggressive.

Causes

The family setting of an unsocialised aggressive child is typically characterised by rejection, harsh and inconsistent discipline and general frustration. Frequently, the parents are unstable in their marital relationships and emotionally disturbed, providing the child little in the form of consistent guidance, acceptance or affection.

How Does Aggression Increase?

A number of factors are responsible for increasing the child's aggression:

1. **Reinforcement:** When instrumental aggression consistently yields children what they want, it is reinforced. Then they persist with their aggressive behaviour.
2. **Frustration:** Punishment, insult and fear may result in frustration. Aggression is an outlet the children find for such frustration.
3. **Violence on Television and Movies:** TV shows are full of violence. Seeing aggressive characters on TV, children end up imitating them. Watching violence seems to make children willing to hurt people.

TYPICAL CASE HISTORIES

1. **Rajesh** was an unmanageable eight-year-old. Whenever his mother refused to comply with his requests, he was upset. At such times, he would throw temper tantrums and lie down on the

floor, kicking and screaming. His mother usually ignored his behaviour for a few minutes, but gave in to his demands when his tantrums became too difficult to bear. This sequence of agitation and giving in became habitual, particularly when the mother was busy. When she felt rushed and perturbed, she gave in to Rajesh almost immediately.

2. Seven-year-old **Mohan** failed to perform adequately in the classroom. The teacher described him as "withdrawn, shy, oversensitive and unable to make friends or participate in classroom activities". During recess he preferred to remain in the classroom and appeared preoccupied with his thoughts and fantasies. He was poor in reading and other routine school subjects. Psychological assessment showed that he was superior in intelligence but suffered from extreme feelings of inadequacy and a pervasive attitude of "I can't do it".

3. A 14-year-old, **Madhuri** ran away with a boy and returned home about a week later. Investigations revealed that the girl was having difficulty in school adjustment and was living in a family situation torn by bickering and dissension. In explaining why she ran away from home, she stated: "I just couldn't take all that quarrelling and criticism any more and no one really cared anyway."

4. **Rakesh** walked in his sleep thrice a week on an average. His sleep-walking episodes were associated with nightmares, perspiring and talking. Psychological assessment showed that just before each sleep-walking episode, Rakesh usually had a nightmare about being chased

by a dog. In his dream, Rakesh thought that the dog would eat his leg. After the onset of his nightmare, he used to perspire, moan and talk in his sleep. Then he tossed and turned, and finally got up and walked through the house. In the morning, he could never recall his sleep-walking. Rakesh was of normal intelligence. However, he was found to be a very anxious, guilt-ridden little boy.

ooo

4

Ways to Improve Children

BEHAVIOUR MODIFICATION TECHNIQUES

These techniques deal primarily with how to change overt student behaviour. This involves application of operant learning principles to bring about a specific change in behaviour.

The operant conditioning aims at getting a desired response from the person on whom it is being applied. Once the desired response occurs, it is reinforced to increase the frequency of its occurrence. This conditioning is also called instrumental conditioning.

Although behaviour modification originated as a technique based on operant conditioning, combinations of behavioural and cognitive approach are now the commonly used methods to bring about behavioural change. Operant conditioning methods use schedules of reinforcement and shaping to gradually achieve a desired response. Special prompts may be employed to highlight a situation that calls for a particular response.

Positive reinforcers such as praise and money are used to strengthen the desired responses. Token economies are special systems based on reinforcement principles, although they have not been as successful in raising the academic levels as they are reported to be in controlling social behaviour. In a token system, a unit of exchange (gift voucher, coupon, IOU slip, credit voucher and so on) is delivered contingent on a specified response. The token acquires the properties of a conditioned reinforcer, which can later be exchanged for a backup reinforcer, usually selected from various items, since in children what constitutes a reinforcer is idiosyncratic. Token reinforcement contingent on academic behaviour has been successfully used to improve academic performance.

Extinction procedure and punishment might be used to eliminate undesirable responses. When punishment is employed to eliminate a response, it is a good idea to simultaneously reinforce an alternative, more desirable, positive response. When no longer needed, gradual elimination of these unwanted behaviours is called fading.

Play and Family Therapy

Play Therapy and Family Therapy are two general methods of treating childhood problems. Generally, children are more reluctant than older people to voice their concerns and complaints directly and openly.

It is assumed that in play therapy a child will express his or her feelings about problems, parents, teachers and peers. This helps the adult therapist establish rapport with a youngster. A play-therapy room is equipped with puppets, blocks, games, puzzles, drawing materials, paints, water, sand, clay, toy guns, soldiers and a large inflated rubber clown to punch. These toys help children vent their inner tension and concerns.

Children usually live with parents and siblings, with whom their lives are inextricably linked. Therefore, therapists examine and attempt to alter the pattern of interaction in families, rather than treating the troubled child or young adolescent alone.

The child's problem has been caused or is sustained by disturbed relationships within the family. For example, the father may have abdicated his responsibilities.

The Importance of Token Economies

Approval and other intangible reinforcers often prove ineffective in behaviour therapy, especially ones dealing with severely maladaptive behaviour. In such instances, appropriate behaviours may be rewarded with tangible reinforcers in the form of tokens that can later be exchanged for desired objects or privileges.

The rules of the token economy are carefully framed and explained to the child. These clearly state the medium of exchange; the small routine tasks like eating, self-care etc. to be rewarded and by what number of tokens; the items and privileges that can be purchased, and for how many tokens.

The number of tokens earned by the child can be equated with the degree of desired behaviour that he manifests; the number of tokens earned and the way they are spent are largely up to the child. These tokens tend to bridge the gap between the institutional environment and the demands and rewards encountered in the outside world.

The ultimate goal is not only to achieve the desired responses but to bring such responses to a level where their adaptive consequences will be reinforcing in their own right, thus enabling natural circumstances rather than artificial reward contingencies to maintain the desired behaviour.

The Child's Emotional Growth

Emotional development begins early in life and stems from the generalised, undifferentiated reactions of the infant to stimulating situations.

These situations differ from child to child but are usually related at first to his physical well-being. The generalised responses become more diversified and specific as the child learns to discriminate between experiences and situations that give him satisfaction and those that do not.

We generally find two types of emotional behaviour: the pleasant or integrative feelings, and the unpleasant or disintegrative feelings. Rage, fear, jealousy, and disgust are considered disintegrative feelings; joy, elation, affection, delight and hope are termed integrative feelings. Both types of behaviour vary in degree or amount of response according to the individual and the situation experienced. If either type of emotions were carried to such an extreme that it became the dominating response regardless of the stimulus, disorganisation of the individual would result. Society places a high premium on integrative responses and attempts are made to minimise disintegrative responses, except in isolated periods of environmental stress such as war, criminal action and so forth.

When the infant's physical needs are cared for, he is warm and satisfied. This feeling of well-being is first associated with the acts that produce the feeling and subsequently with the people performing the acts. As the child matures, he discovers ways of causing the pleasant action to occur. When he succeeds, his basic sense of trust is enhanced. When events do not happen as his experiences have taught him to expect, he becomes confused and uncertain about his environment and also about his own responses. Thus he develops a pattern of response that works in most situations to obtain the desired result. When he is unsuccessful in coping with a particular situation, or when he has no preconceived response, unpleasant emotions such as fear and anger follow, contributing to the feeling of distrust.

As children gain in intellectual abilities, in physical and motor skills, and in awareness of the significance of their environment, they acquire emotional reactions and patterns appropriate to their level of development and their experiences. The four-year-old child tends to be afraid of the dark, goblins and ghosts, while the 12-year-old is afraid of such things like school failure, tardiness and not being liked by others.

Under essentially the same conditions, two children will react quite differently due to their emotional growth. For example, one child expresses joy and pleasure at being able to hold a kitten, while another moves back in fear and refuses any physical contact with it.

Some investigators have claimed that emotion is hereditary and instinctual; others feel that it begins as a physiological reaction; still others emphasise the environment as the source of differentiated emotional response.

When children engage in actions that are not easily understood, that are less common and more surprising, we call them emotionally disturbed children.

The Importance of Motor Development

The development of motor skills is essential for participation in group activities during childhood. Many informal social contacts centre on the performance of motor activities. The child who does not achieve proficiency in skills like cycling, ball playing, skipping and gymnastics is likely to be left on the fringe of group activities.

Successful learning of motor skills has an effect on personality development. Children gain personal satisfaction and a feeling of achievement from well-executed physical activities and the ability to compete successfully with others. Motor achievement leads to social status among peers and greater group acceptance.

Good motor skills aid personality development

Before skills can be learned the child must be mature. Once maturation is reached, the opportunity to practise and the attitudes of the people with whom the child associates are important factors in determining the degree of skill acquired. Parents can encourage children to learn by showing interest in and enthusiasm about his performance. While it may be necessary to set physical limits for the safety of the child, an overprotective attitude or undue concern may discourage his initiative and interest in motor activities.

Equipment that encourages practice in both gross and fine body movements should be made available to children. Between the ages of five and eight, most children need experience in the use of large muscles. Running, climbing and jumping games are not only popular but also foster co-ordination and efficiency of movement.

Opportunities to practise fine motor skills, such as hammering, sawing, drawing and cutting with scissors, are also important. But these activities require more refined coordination and will be performed more skilfully by 10- and 11-year-olds. Young children are more interested in learning how to use the tools than in the finished product.

Teaching Social and Personal Skills

Behaviour is the result of a person's interaction with his environment. Repeated behaviour of the same type occurs because of the individual's expectation that the environment will in some way reinforce the behaviour that is of value to him.

While studying this complex process, psychologists have attempted to alter, manipulate or control the environment in various ways in an effort to modify an individual's behaviour. The term *behaviour modification* has been used to describe this approach.

A child's behaviour is changed by consequent parental reaction to it. If you provide a child with something he wants after he has behaved in a certain way, that behaviour will increase. If you withhold the reinforcer, the behaviour will eventually disappear. If you punish the child, the undesired behaviour will decrease immediately but will probably recur soon.

The immediacy with which the reinforcer is applied and the degree to which you are consistent with the consequence are both important considerations. After a behaviour has become established, it can be maintained by reinforcing once in a while or adopting a gambling schedule where the child never knows when he will receive the reinforcer and so tries harder and longer in anticipation of the reward.

You must also be careful not to expect too much from a child at the very beginning. Otherwise, you would end up never reinforcing him because he could not reach a higher goal set by you.

Remember – reinforce successive approximations to the goal but never reward the child when he returns to the level of performance he had already attained.

Caution should be exercised so that undesirable behaviour is not rewarded. This occurs frequently, particularly in cases involving discipline. Many children seek attention by misbehaving all too frequently. Teachers as well as parents reward misbehaviour by calling attention to it. And, children seeking attention are reinforced in this behaviour. In most instances, the preferred technique for handling a social or behaviour problem is to ignore the person misbehaving. Certain reprehensible circumstances require that the child be removed from the environment or administered some type of punishment. Attempts should always be made to remove the possibility of the child being rewarded for misbehaviour.

In their efforts to help children understand and develop satisfactory social, personal and emotional behaviour, parents and teachers often lecture children about how and why they are to behave in a certain fashion. Even with the best of intentions, this method of instruction will have only minimal impact for several reasons. First, lecturing assumes that the children have developed language and conceptual skills needed to understand abstract notions. Secondly, lecturing is a poor strategy since it does not provide the children opportunities to look at themselves and evaluate their own performance. Each child must be given opportunities to engage in activities that will help him evaluate the reasons for and against behaving in a certain fashion under various circumstances.

An acceptable pattern of behaviour will be most

rapidly and effectively acquired under the dual influence of models and differential reinforcement. Children will value and reflect the behaviour of models they consider to be of high credibility. Moreover, they will react more favourably to the reinforcement provided by these "high-credibility" individuals than to those dispensed by a "low-credibility person".

Parents will find that the behaviour of children can be dramatically changed and subsequently controlled when models are used in ways that allow for imitation by youngsters.

Role of Punishment

Most parents perceive punishment as an effective corrective measure against their children's undesirable behaviour. All parents use it occasionally. But parents should bear in mind that, in comparison with punishment, reinforcement is most effective in building new patterns of behaviour.

The effects of punishment are suppressive. When punishment works, it reduces the likelihood of certain noxious or potentially dangerous responses. Punishment should always be administered in ways that have some significance for the child.

Time is very important in the naturalistic use of punishment against the young child. Acting in an extremely antisocial way, if a child hits a younger sibling, steals, resorts to lying or commits an act of vandalism, some time will inevitably pass before the transgression is detected. Even after detection, an extended waiting period may be present before potential punishment, as is evident in the familiar warning, *Wait till your father comes home.* It is therefore important to determine the relationship between the timing of punishment and its effectiveness.

As a rule, mild punishment will be maximally effective

if it is meted out immediately after the deviant act or while the act is occurring.

Remember that the punishment will be much less effective if its application is considerably delayed after the occurrence of the deviant act. Delayed punishment will be confusing in its purpose, at least for very young children.

If parents punish their child in the evening for a transgression committed in the morning, a situation may be created in which the child may show negative consequences after his desirable behaviour which the parents otherwise would have wished to encourage and reinforce.

Explain the reason for punishment to increase effectiveness

Punishment from a parent who is usually rewarding and nurturing towards the child is likely to be more effective than the same punishment from one who is usually cold and distant. Adults who practise what they preach are likely to be more effective in their reprimands than those who do not. Parents who follow punishment with a display of affection towards the errant children may counteract the impact of the punishment and will probably strengthen the undesirable response.

When punishment is used, it is desirable that the

child learns another response to substitute the one for which he was punished. For example, if a child fights frequently, his tendency to fight should be reduced and get substituted after punishment.

Explaining the reason for punishment increases its effectiveness. Reasoning and explanation play a very important role in the development of self-control among older children. These help children evaluate their own behaviour by explaining exactly what activity should be avoided and why.

Fostering Creativity

Training fosters creativity. It is possible to train a child to develop creativity. If freedom of exploration and decision is granted to a child, he starts moving towards creativity. The child should be suitably rewarded and encouraged for his new achievements. He should be allowed to develop without undue pressure. It should also be kept in mind that children with loving parents tend to accept parental attitudes and thus become somewhat conformist in nature. Parents who are unreasonable or too rigid, on the other hand, may encourage a rebellious attitude in their children that will lead to independent thinking and action.

Always remember that rewards can play a vital role in developing many aspects of behaviour. Incentives can increase children's creativity. But in all likelihood such training will produce only moderate changes in their creative performance.

The main components of creativity are: cognition involving discovery, awareness, recognition, comprehension or understanding; memory, involving retention and storage of information; divergent thinking, which involves the generation of information from the given information; convergent thinking, where the emphasis is on the use of the given information to produce the best response; and evaluation, or reaching decisions or making judgements concerning the correctness, suitability, adequacy, and desirability of information in terms of criteria of identity, consistency, and goal satisfaction.

ooo

5

Influence of the Environment on Children

Impact of Divorce on Children

Children who live with their divorced mothers, especially boys, face more social, academic and behavioural problems. A number of factors influence children's adjustment to the fallout of divorce and their adjustment with society. These include:

(a) **Parenting Style and Satisfaction:** Children of authoritative divorced parents show fewer problems at school and with other children. With those parents who are able to control their anger, children have fewer emotional and social problems.

(b) **Remarriage of the Mother:** Remarriage demands adjustment. Research studies have shown that remarried mothers tend to be happier, better adjusted and more satisfied with life. Their sons do better with the stepfather, but daughters have more problems than the daughters of divorced mothers who have not remarried.

(c) **Relationship with Father:** In adolescent boys whose parents had divorced ten years ago, the relationship with the father influences their post-divorce adjustment with the mother. The sons of erratic and rejecting fathers feel humiliated and hurt and often react with anger against their mothers.

(d) **Accessibility of Both Parents:** Predictable and frequent contact with the parent who is not easily accessible is most important. The typical practice of limited visitation for fathers deprives children of the desired love and protection. This acts like rejection.

Influence of the Employed Mother

Research studies have been undertaken to find out how the mother's employment influences the child's performance and personality. The findings show that the employed mother feels more competent, more economically secure and more in command of her children's lives. Her self-esteem tends to be higher than that of unemployed mothers. She is more satisfied with life and more effective as a parent.

In a family where the mother is working, the division of work is less traditional. The father is more involved in the children's upbringing and household work than his counterpart in the families of non-working mothers. He is most involved when his wife has a full-time job and they have more than one child. The involved father shows nurturing by expressing love, helping children with their concerns and problems through care and attention. This is not the case with fathers in non-working mothers' families; with working mothers and involved fathers, children have fewer stereotypes about gender roles.

School-age children of employed women have two advantages over children of non-employed mothers. They tend to live in more structured homes with clear-cut rules and household responsibilities. They are more encouraged to be independent. This makes the children, especially daughters, feel more competent to achieve more in school and have higher self-esteem. Daughters of working mothers tend to be more independent and have a more positive attitude towards being a female than those of mothers who are at home.

Sibling's Influence

Siblings influence each other directly through their interaction and indirectly through their impact on each other's relationship with the parents. Siblings' interaction with each other helps them develop self-confidence. Children learn a lot of new things from their brothers and/or sisters. They also learn to resolve conflicts. Though they may quarrel, they know that it will not mean the end of the relationship. Compromise, negotiations and being sensitive to the other's needs are skills they learn through conflicts.

First-borns tend to be dominating and the younger ones tend to be more skilful in resolving conflicts. Interdependence, caretaking and nurturing constitute other aspects of social skills that siblings learn through mutual interaction. Elder girls explain more to younger siblings than boys do. Older brothers tend to be more aggressive and bossy in their attitude.

Why Children like Comics

While reading comics, children find an escape from their real environment. The comic allows the child to identify himself with an all-powerful and always right hero. On reaching the last stage of childhood, the child is able to give up comics as his tastes and abilities mature.

However, it would not be correct to assume that maturity occurs only when comics have been given up. In many ways, comics reflect the changing times of our society. One can hardly assume that to continue reading comics is a hallmark of immaturity. Children ultimately find that comics do not meet their needs for aesthetically pleasing material. They also find that the material is highly unrealistic in relation to their everyday problems. At this time, they are ready to move towards more realistic stories or books.

Give him space of his own

For many children, comics become a "coin of the realm" – they can be bartered for marbles and other tokens of value for the child. As the child matures, the value of this material tends to diminish.

There is a body of evidence to reassure parents and teachers about the effects of comics upon school-going children. On comparing children who read a lot of comics with those who read them rarely, it was found that both groups had the same intelligence levels. Although individual reading patterns varied a great deal, some children classed as 'comic readers' had excellent overall reading programmes. There were no distinguishing characteristics that marked readers or non-readers of comics.

The child who feels a need to be delinquent, or to escape from the demands of life, appears to find comics useful. Comics seem to be the most readily obtainable means to help him achieve his end. When the child reads any comic, he is exposed to many new words that increase his vocabulary.

There are many reasons why comics appeal to children. They are readily available, inexpensive, rely on a simple and exciting story line and are profusely and colourfully illustrated. The print is generally large and the books are short. They become barter material, too.

Goal-directed Behaviour

Parents should always bear in mind that the behaviour of children is often goal directed and the result of a desire to satisfy needs. These needs are the result of the normal interaction that takes place between an individual and his environment. These needs do not evolve only in a person's mind, or result from the environment alone, their origin is a consequence of the environment-individual mix. Certain goals are highly positive, and the need for achieving them is high. Other goals are not positive. For example, because of peer pressure a child may have an intense desire to learn cycling, whereas he may not view book learning with the same degree of positiveness.

We often feel frustrated in achieving goals when the necessary repertoire of skills has not been developed. The main needs of the child are attention, affection, activity, acceptance and success. When one is thwarted in achieving a goal, he can either make another frontal attack, attempting to penetrate or circumvent the barriers or, after repeated failures, he can search for a reasonable substitute for the goals that he finds unattainable through direct means.

To reduce tension, an individual must either achieve his goal or engage in some type of socially accepted and situationally appropriate alternate behaviour.

INFANT'S EMOTIONS

Infants show their emotions in different ways. When an infant is uncomfortable, he cries, stiffens his body and flings his arms and legs around. When the baby is happy, he shows it through different expressions. During the first month when infants become quiet on hearing a human voice or when they are picked up, they smile. When their hands are moved together in play, they smile, coo, reach out and eventually move towards people. All these are signs and reliable clues of the baby's emotions.

When they need something, they cry; when they feel sociable, they laugh and smile. Their sense of personal power grows as they see that their cries bring help and comfort, and their smiles and laughter elicit a similar response from others. But these emotional expressions convey different meanings as the baby grows. At first, crying is a signal of physical discomfort; later on, it expresses psychological distress.

Here is a brief description of an infant's specific emotions:

Crying

There are four crying patterns: the basic hunger cry, the anger cry, the pain cry, and the frustration cry. The hunger cry is rhythmic, and the anger cry has a variation of rhythm. The pain cry is often sudden and loud, while the frustration cry is accompanied by two or three drawn-out cries without prolonged holding of the breath.

An infant's cry must be responded to with care and tenderness. If the mothers do so, their infants cry less by the time they are a year old, compared to those whose cries were not responded to quickly by their mothers.

Smiling

The first smile occurs soon after birth, as a result of central nervous system (CNS) activity, often when the baby is asleep. In the second week, babies often smile after getting their feed. When they are drowsy they may be responding to the caregiver's sounds. Later, smiles come more often when the babies are alert but inactive.

After about one month, the baby's smiles become frequent and more social. They smile when their hands are clapped together or when they hear a familiar voice. During the second month, they become more receptive to people whom they already know.

Laughter

Babies start laughing around the fourth month. Some of their laughter may be related to fear because sometimes they react with the same stimulus to both fear and laughter. As they grow older, they respond to sounds and cough and may be delighted by games at seven to nine months. This shift reflects cognitive development. Laughter is a response to the environment, which helps babies discharge tension in situations that otherwise might be upsetting. Laughter represents an important relationship between cognitive development and emotional development.

EFFECTS OF TV ON CHILDREN'S BEHAVIOUR

Some time or the other everyone shows aggression in a way that brings discomfort to others. The type of aggression that a person displays and his ability to control such actions change significantly with age and experience.

Many parents feel that their children are more likely to become aggressive when they are upset, agitated or excited. Research has shown that emotional arousal does appear to influence a child's willingness to become aggressive and that the process may operate differently in boys and girls. Overall, the level of aggression is more in boys than in girls.

Excessive viewing of violence on television could make your child aggressive

Although children may be provoked into aggression by irritating or provoking events in their environment, most aggressive acts also have a basis in the child's past learning history. Youngsters usually follow aggressive behaviour or those who have come across a number of aggressive models are prone to learn aggressive behaviour that can be easily activated whenever provocations occur. Children can also learn ways of behaving aggressively by merely watching others indulging in such behaviour, no matter that the aggressive model is punished for such hostile behaviour.

The same principles apply to the television model of aggression. Therefore, serious questions have been raised about the portrayal of violence in children's television programmes. Youngsters could learn novel aggressive responses from television and television-like formats. Research findings show that the more the child watches violence on TV, the more aggressive he is likely to be.

Findings of UNESCO Study

According to a report published in *The Hindustan Times*, a survey was conducted in 2000 about acts of violence aired on TV. After studying five channels for nine days through 759 acts of telly violence, Zee topped the chart and Doordarshan had the least telly violence.

Zee TV's 'scorecard' had registered 365 points against DD's 62. Star TV was number two with a score of 188 and Sony had 64 points. Interestingly, DD II's violence ratings at 80 were higher than Sony's.

According to a study conducted by UNESCO, *X-Zone* and *Anhonee* on Zee were found to have a higher degree of violence, compared to *Kohra* on Star Plus and *Aahat* on Sony.

Making a clear distinction between audio and visual violence, the study categorised eerie soundtrack and threatening music to be audio violence against visual violence that included shooting, assaulting and stabbing, amongst other acts of violence. In addition to the excessive depiction of murder, bombing and burning, many serials depict verbal abuse, bizarre sound effects and, occasionally, psychological violence.

Even when care was taken to avoid acts of physical violence, certain serials repeatedly used hallucinations, nightmares and paranoia for an effective build up of an atmosphere of terror, the study noted.

Yet, more than the violent content, what was really disturbing was the trend of horror shows and crime serials to target the child viewer. Surveys indicate that children eagerly watch many of these programmes.

Adjustive Mechanisms to Release Tension

Each of us has a certain moment by moment tolerance level against frustration and tension. When this level is reached or exceeded, there is a need for tension to be released through some type of adjustive or defensive behaviour. Then, the choice before an individual is to use any type of behaviour to protect his integrity, if he fails to achieve his goal and feels frustrated.

Behaviours such as classified aggression, substitution, withdrawal, projection, suppression and reaction formation come under the category of adjustive mechanisms, when people choose to relieve their tension.

These mechanisms are defined below:

Aggression : Behaviour aimed at hurting someone or destroying something.

Substitution : Acceptance or satisfaction with substitute goals in place of those originally sought or desired.

Withdrawal : Intellectual, emotional or physical retreat.

Projection : Ego-defence mechanism in which individual attributes his own unacceptable desires and impulses to others.

Suppression : Conscious inhibition of desire or impulses.

Reaction Formation : Ego-defence mechanism in which individual's conscious attitudes and overt behaviour are the opposite of his repressed subconscious wishes.

We know that an individual's view of his own capabilities and level of achievement is based to a large degree on his history of success and failure within a given environment.

For example, if a child has not had an opportunity to succeed in school activities and constantly failed, he will develop a complex network of antagonisms towards those activities. This may result in the youngster eventually exhibiting a general dislike for anything associated with school. He will begin to view himself as inadequate and may even develop a dislike for or become hostile towards authority figures, such as teachers.

ooo

6

Helping Children Develop Basic Skills

Methods of Learning

Three basic methods of learning are widely recognised:
1. Classical conditioning
2. Instrumental learning
3. Observational learning

Classical Conditioning: From infancy onwards children learn many attitudes and much behaviour through classical conditioning, including negative and positive evaluations, fears, and prejudices. The Russian psychologist Pavlov and the American psychologist Watson proved it experimentally. In one such experiment, a child named Albert was conditioned to fear a mat.

Classical conditioning is also called respondent conditioning. It is a basic form of learning in which a previously neutral stimulus comes to elicit a given response.

Instrumental Learning: Also called operant conditioning, in this type of learning the subject is reinforced for making a predetermined response, such as pressing a lever. It is based on Thorndike's original law of effect, which states that the consequences of an act determine the probability of its future occurrence. Positive and negative reinforcement increases the probability of occurrence, whereas punishment decreases it.

As in classical conditioning, extinction, generalisation and discrimination are relevant to instrumental learning. Extinction occurs when a response that once led to reinforcement no longer does so. Generalisation of the learned response occurs when individuals exhibit the act in situations that are similar but not identical to the setting in which reinforcement occurred in the past.

Discrimination means that individuals are able to distinguish settings from the earlier setting when the reinforcement took place.

Observational Learning: This is a function of viewing the behaviour of others. Its possible effects consist of direct imitation and counter-imitation as well as inhibition and disinhibition, both of which involve generalisation. Observation learning occurs in three steps:
- i) Exploration
- ii) Acquisition
- iii) Acceptance

Parents should always bear in mind that children must see a reason for participation in any activity. Children can be stimulated and appropriately rewarded, which leads to their becoming eager or motivated to engage in an activity and to acquire certain associated skills.

A Developmental Schedule

By the age of around six years, 70 percent of children become homolateral, i.e. they have established dominant use of one side of the body. This dominance is consistent for hand, foot, ear and eye. The remaining 30 percent will be cross lateral throughout their lives.

The most important feature of cross laterality is a dominant left eye with a dominant right hand, or a dominant right eye alongside a dominant left hand. Most intelligent people can cope adequately with cross laterality and are usually unaware that they possess this feature of development.

However, according to available evidence, cross laterality is a handicap during the period of learning to read and write for the less able amongst us, particularly those who are slow to mature.

MAIN DEVELOPMENT NORMS

An average five-year-old is able to stand on tiptoe for five seconds. An average six-year-old can stand on one foot with the other raised behind from the knee for 15 seconds, hop on one foot for five metres and walk heel to toe along a strip line or rail for ten steps.

For ball throwing at a target which lies at a distance of three metres:

a) The above-average five-year-old will hit on or near a target on three occasions.
b) The average five-year-old will hit the wall.
c) The below-average five-year-old will be "way out" in the attempt.

Bead Stringing: The six-year-old should thread at least eight beads in 25 seconds.

Visual Achievement Forms: If the child is unable to copy the number of forms appropriate for his age, he is unlikely to be able to read by the look-say method without further preparation. He is also unlikely to be able to write with reasonable legibility.

a) Children of seven years should be able to copy all forms.
b) Children of six years should be able to copy five forms.

c) Children of five years should be able to copy four forms.

d) Children of four years should be able to copy three forms.

Please note how the child copies the forms.

Visual Memory: The child who cannot remember the relative positions of three toys is unlikely to build a basic sight vocabulary.

Drawing Person: The ability to draw a recognisable man or woman has much to offer as a diagnostic tip to parents and teachers. Drawing at five or six years of age seems to come from within the child's experience, rather than it being a copy of a person. Even if there is a person standing directly ahead of the child, he shows no indication of observing and drawing that figure. Achievement of this task is also related to laterality (experience of sidedness) and later on to the ability to discriminate between 'b' and 'd', 'u' and 'n', 'was' and 'saw', 'on' and 'no' and general spellings.

In the following figures, the children's "Drawing-a-Man" have been classified into five categories, A to E, according to the fineness of their sketches.

Drawing-a-Man Test: The scoring of the Drawing-a-Man Test consists essentially of assigning each drawing to an appropriate category, in accordance with the criteria outlined below.

Category	Essential Characteristics
B : *Above Average*	In addition to characteristics given in E, D and C, most of the following: Arms and legs in two dimensions. Better proportion (length of trunk greater than breadth). Clothing clearly indicated. More detail, such as eyebrows and pupils.

A : *Superior*	In addition to characteristics given in E, D, C and B, most of the following: Clothing non-transparent.

Lines firm and meeting at proper points.

Such detail as neck, hands, shoulders and correct number of fingers.

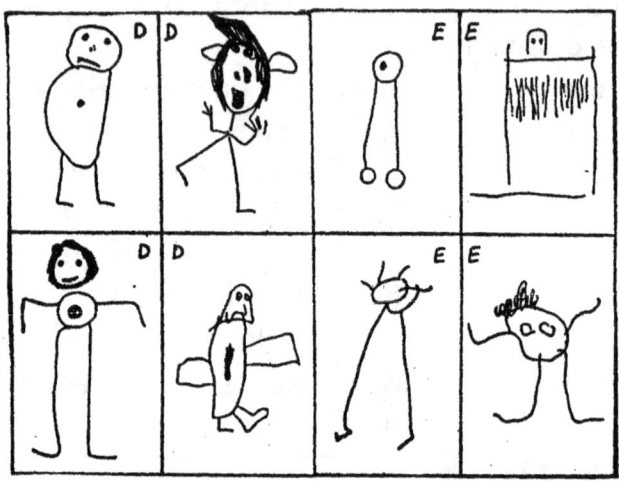

D : *Below Average* In addition to features given under E, most of the following:

Arms in one dimension only.

Trunk, mouth, nose, and hair.

C : *Average* In addition to characteristics given in D and E, most of the following:

Fingers, ears, and nostrils.

Some proportion among parts.

E : *Immature* Figure not recognisable as a human being.

Parts of body not connected, such as eyes, legs, outline of head.

Common Words in Children's Books

These words should never be taught as a list, but used whenever possible in meaningful contexts. Some may perhaps be used in reading games, or introduced when the child is making his own reading book. Alternatively, the list may be used in specific cases for diagnostic purposes. Some practical suggestions for use will be given during this course.

Twelve words make up, on average, one-quarter of all reading. These are as follows:

a	and	he	I	in	is	it	of	that	the
				to	was				

The following 20 words together with the above 12 words (32 words) make up, on average, one-third of all reading:

all	as	at	be	but	are
for	had	have	him	his	not
on	one	said	so	they	we
		with	you		

The following 68 words together with the above 32 words (100 words) make up, on average, one-half of all reading:

about	an	back	been	before	big	by	all	came
can	come	could	did	do	down	first	from	get
go	has	her	here	if	into	just	like	little
look	made	make	more	me	much	must	my	no
new	now	off	old	only	or	our	other	out
over	right	see	she	some	their	them	then	there
this	two	up	want	well	went	were	what	when
where	which	who	will	your				

The next 100 most used words. Nouns underlined:

after	again	always	come	another	any	ask	away
bad	because	best	<u>bird</u>	black	blue	<u>boy</u>	bring
<u>day</u>	<u>dog</u>	don't					
eat	every						

far   fast   <u>father</u>   fell   find   five   fly   four   found
gave   girl   give   going   good   got   green   <u>hand</u>   have   <u>head</u>   help   <u>home</u>   <u>house</u>   how   jump
keep   know
last   left   let   live   long
<u>man</u>   many   may   <u>men</u>   <u>mother</u>   Mr
never   next
once   open   own
play   put
ran   read   red   room   round   run
sat   saw   say   <u>school</u> should sing   sit   soon   stop
take   tell   than   these   <u>thing</u>   think   three   <u>time</u>   toot   <u>tree</u>
under   us
very
walk   white   why   wish   work   would   <u>year</u>

Fifty additional nouns

apple	baby	bag	ball	bed
book	box	bus	car	cat
children	cow	cup	dinner	doll
door	egg	end	farm	fish
fun	hat	hill	horse	jam
letter	milk	money	morning	Mrs
name	night	nothing	picture	pig
place	rabbit	road	sea	shop
sister	street	sun	table	tea
today	top	toy	train	water

These 250 words make up approximately 70% of juvenile reading and about 60% of adult reading.

DEVELOPING SKILLS IN WRITTEN COMMUNICATION

Handwriting

Children must have a certain minimal level of muscular coordination. They must be able to grasp a pencil or piece of chalk and maintain a certain posture while it is manipulated.

Initially, children should be given experiences that allow them to practise the basic writing movements. They can be made to draw a configuration of circles and straight and slanted lines by giving them freedom of movement in art and drawing. At the very outset, it is unwise to force children to do small motor tasks with a pencil or pen until they have first practised the strokes on a blackboard or a large piece of paper with a soft pencil, felt pen, chalk or crayon.

Gradually, as they develop control, children are taught to combine their circles and other strokes, formerly used for drawing, into the formation of letters and words. Full attention should be given to the development of a clear image of the letter and an appropriate sequence for making the strokes. Paper with horizontal lines is recommended for this stage. Accuracy and not speed should always be stressed. Care should be exercised so that children focus on the total configuration of the letter, rather than the line segments being traced when they are asked to trace the letters.

Proceed from the simple to the complex by introducing lowercase letters in the following sequence: l, e, i, t, u, n, m, h, k, w, o, b, v, x, y, j, f, s, p, r, e, a, d, g, q, z.

Capital letters can be taught as the need arises, such as when a name is written.

Spelling

As in any subject area involving the use of complex skills, expectations for spelling achievement will vary according to the unique weaknesses an individual child exhibits. For example, children with visualisation difficulties may have substantial problems in spelling. Similarly, children with auditory discrimination problems could have spelling weaknesses because they may be unable to hear the sounds peculiar to spelling words.

The fundamental skills required for learning spellings are:
1. Auditory and visual reception
2. Auditory and visual memory
3. Auditory and visual discrimination
4. Association of auditory and visual stimuli
5. Motor expression
6. Vocal expression

Because English has such a confusing phonetic structure, teaching spelling by rules will be less effective and more confusing.

Written Expression

Too much direct emphasis on grammatical structure and other technical aspects of writing should not constitute a large segment of the programme. Children should be exposed to a good model. Emphasis should be placed on inter-relating oral and written communication.

Main Reading Skills

The reading process is exceedingly complicated. An individual must master a series of complex skills to effectively perform and receive the maximum advantage from reading. Adequate reception, discrimination among sounds and symbols, association among various components involved in reading, remembering a visual and auditory sequence, understanding material, applying facts and concepts to earlier learned material and the effective expression of ideas comprise some of the major factors involved in reading.

The complexities involved in adequate mastery of these skills provide a reasonable explanation why some children often encounter great difficulty in learning to read. The added ambition of helping them to develop a conceptual instead of rote competency only increases the magnitude of the problem.

The main reading readiness skills are:
1. Discriminating among sounds and visual displays
2. Remembering an auditory or visual sequence
3. Listening for details
4. Following directions
5. Recognising letters
6. Using context for clues to comprehension
7. Eye-hand coordination
8. Seeing relationships
9. Interpreting pictures

Readiness for Arithmetic

The readiness for arithmetic can be viewed from two perspectives. First, adequate arithmetic achievement is fundamentally dependent on the student's ability to discriminate between and remember auditory and visual stimuli, attend to the task, accurately perceive spatial orientation and translate these phenomena into temporal sequences and associate stimuli and express himself.

For rote counting alone, which is a very elementary arithmetic skill, children must listen carefully, perceive accurately, discriminate among sounds, remember the components and their appropriate sequence and vocally or gesturally express the numerical chain. This simple task requires a certain minimum level of achievement in each of these basic areas.

Auditory (Phonic) Readiness

The child who correctly synthesises four or five words is ready for a phonetic approach within his learning to read. The average three-year-old is able to repeat three digits in one out of three trials. The average seven-year-old is able to repeat five digits.

Auditory Sequential Memory

Understanding and carrying out instructions are essential pre-reading skills. Even young children predict (guess) the next word during their reading but they need an adequate memory and understanding before they are able to do this.

Readiness for Learning

When young children enter school, their progress depends to a large extent upon their readiness to learn and upon the provisions the school makes for variations in readiness.

Among the chief factors that contribute to readiness for beginning school work are linguistic attainment and aptitudes, visual and auditory perception, muscular coordination and motor skills, number knowledge, and the ability to follow directions and to pay attention in group work.

How far advanced the school beginner will be in these skills depends upon many factors, such as his intelligence, home background, health and physical condition, degree of emotional maturity and social adjustment, and general background of experience.

Lack of readiness in any of the above traits may account for a child's failure to learn in the first grade.

Among the factors inherent in the concept of readiness is the general belief that a child must be mature enough to respond in a consistent and accurate manner. A child needs to acquire certain basic skills before adequate performance can be expected from him in areas such as walking, drawing, gross and fine motor movements, and other types of visual motor activities. The influence of maturation on verbal skills, and more generally on cognition, is less well validated, since there is larger inter-individual variation in these areas than in non-verbal skills. In order to receive incoming stimuli, engage in associational activities and respond properly, the child must be in a state of attentiveness.

Many believe that general lack of attention is the primary reason that a number of children often do poorly in school. If the necessary basic skills upon which subsequent learning is dependent have not developed, any new skills will at best develop in an inefficient and disorganised manner, often totally out of context.

Reading Readiness

Research findings indicate that for reading readiness in children, it is necessary to lay the foundation for fundamental skills and abilities needed to interpret the printed page. Children who acquire this foundation learn to read better and faster, with less wastage of time and effort. This can prevent many failures in beginning to read.

Basic Skills Required

1. **Auditory Discrimination:** Required to isolate and identify sounds.

2. **Short-term Auditory Memory:** Required for phonetic analysis and synthesis tables and spellings etc.
3. **Auditory Memory for Continuous Material:** For carrying out operations and organising oneself.
4. **Visual Memory:** To recognise the shape of letters and words.
5. **Figure Ground Perception:** (i) For analysis and synthesis of words; (ii) For scanning; and (iii) For use of a dictionary.
6. **Position in Space:** (i) To distinguish between e, g, b, d, was, saw and the like; (ii) To prevent reversals and rotations; (iii) To recognise the sequence of letters in words; and (iv) To undertake arrangement of materials on page.
7. **Visual Motor Co-ordination:** Eye movement is a prerequisite for reading and correct eye-hand movement coordination is required for writing.
8. **Constancy of Shapes:** For identification of forms (words) regardless of size, colour, texture of angle etc.
9. **Auditory-Visual Integration:** For coordination of auditory and visual discrimination

CHECKLIST FOR PARENTS

Assessing the Child's Reading Readiness

It is now recognised that a certain level of maturity is required to support the skill of reading. Children introduced to reading before this readiness is attained often fail and may become frustrated and lack confidence. Such effects are not easily rectified and can permanently discourage a child from reading. This is why care is essential in deciding when formal reading should begin.

What follows are the Tansley and Gulliford guidelines, but teachers should remember that an overall assessment of the pupil is the best basis on which to proceed.

A. Mental Maturity

Mental maturity of 6-6½ is considered the age for reading readiness. But this cannot be taken in isolation. Some children with this level of mental maturity are still not personally or emotionally mature enough to begin formal reading. Others may lack the necessary verbal skills, or may be handicapped by lack of general social experience.

In assessing mental maturity, observe the following points:
1. Is the pupil of a measured mental maturity of 6½-7½?
2. Can the pupil give reasons for his own work or the work of others?
3. Can he draw something, as well as others of his own age, to demonstrate an idea?
4. Can he memorise a short poem or song?
5. Can he repeat accurately a sentence of five or six words?
6. Can he narrate a story without confusing the order of events?
7. Can he dramatise a simple story effectively?
8. Can he listen and work for an average length of time without restlessness?

Mental Habits
9. Has he established good left to right habits in looking at a succession of words?
10. Can he interpret the content of a picture?

11. Can he arrange a series of pictures in correct story sequence?
12. Can he grasp the fact that symbols may be associated with pictures?
13. Can he anticipate what may happen in a story or poem?
14. Can he remember the central thought as well as important details?

B. Background of Experience

This is the area that provides the interest and knowledge upon which the teaching of reading may be based. It includes the child's language development and verbal skills, as well as his general attitude to reading.

Attitude to Reading

15. Does the pupil appear to be interested in books and reading?
16. Does he ask the meaning of words and signs?
17. Is he interested in the shapes of unusual words?
18. Does he realise that information may be obtained from books?

Verbal Skills

19. Does the pupil speak clearly?
20. Does he speak correctly after being helped with some difficulty?
21. Does he speak in sentences?
22. Does he understand the words of a First Reader when they are used in speech?
23. Does he know certain related words, such as: up/down, big/little, top/bottom, when used in speech?

Good Listening
24. Is the pupil attentive to the spoken word?
25. Does he listen rather than interrupt?
26. Does he listen to an entire story he enjoys so that he can retell all or some of it?
27. Can he follow simple directions?

C. Social Readiness

Learning to read usually takes place in a group setting, so a child's readiness for group participation must be assessed and fostered. Qualities of persistence, concentration, self-reliance and independence are also important.

Cooperation
28. Does the pupil work well in the group and take his share of responsibility?
29. Does he cooperate in games with other children?
30. Does he show a cooperative attitude towards the teacher?

Sharing
31. Does the pupil share class materials without monopolising them?
32. Does he wait for his turn in play and games?
33. Does he willingly wait for his turn when the teacher is checking work?

Self-reliance
34. Does the pupil try to work things out for himself before seeking help?
35. Does he take reasonable care of his clothing and materials?
36. Can he find something constructive to do when he finishes an assigned task?

D. Emotional Readiness

"Premature attempts to teach basic reading formally before the child has enough self-control to focus his emotional energies on the task of learning may defeat their object..." (Tansley and Gulliford). It appears that considering adjustment to tasks and general points best assesses this aspect of readiness.

Adjustment to Task

37. Does the pupil see a task through to completion? Informal drawing or clearing up work provides good observation on this point.
38. Does he accept changes in school or class routine with reasonable calm?
39. Does he appear well adjusted to school work and behave with a relaxed attitude, display pride in work, and an eagerness for new tasks?

Poise

40. Does the pupil accept opposition or defeat without sulking, withdrawal or aggression?
41. Does he meet strangers without undue shyness?
42. Does he meet them without becoming over-familiar?

E. Specific Abilities

Visual Readiness

This attribute not only requires the ability to perceive and discriminate shapes, but also the ability to remember their significance. The degree of visual readiness required for reading appears to vary. Some intelligent pupils with cerebral palsy learn to read quite well, even though showing marked disturbance on visual Gestalt tests.

It has been found, however, that there is a relationship between a child's ability to copy certain standard figures and a successful start to formal reading. The figures are shown in item 43 and the figures in brackets indicate the ages at which children who are developing normally should be able to copy the figures with reasonable accuracy:

43. Can the pupil copy the following figures?

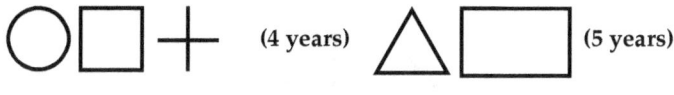

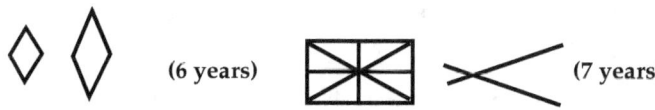

Visual Retention

44. Can the pupil reproduce the following patterns if these are shown for 15 seconds?

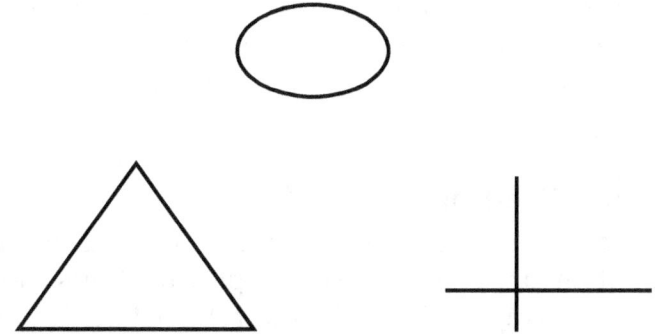

Visual Discrimination

45. Can the pupil match and copy shapes? The examples are from the Visual Discrimination & Orientation Test, Standard Reading Tests (Daniels & Diack).

If a pupil has difficulty with this example, the whole test should be given.

46. Can he interpret a picture without paying too much attention to irrelevant background details?
47. Can he see similarities and differences in letters and words?
    b-d   p-q   m-n   t-l   g-j   j-y
    top-tap pot-pat now-won bit-lit   no-on
48. Can he pick out a word, thread, from similar words after 15 seconds' exposure?
    Choose from: thred   thread
    threab   thread   threed   threard

Auditory Readiness

Inaccurate speech, inattention during oral lessons and frequent misunderstanding of simple directions may all indicate hearing difficulty in a pupil. Such deficiencies are more easily overlooked than visual deficiencies and teachers should be alert to them.

Where such adverse signs are present, the opinion of an audiometrist is required. Even when an examination shows that there are no hearing defects, some pupils may still be unable to discriminate speech sounds adequately. The level of auditory discrimination required for initial reading programmes is not high unless phonics are included at an early stage.

49. Is the pupil able to follow what is said by the teacher, or other pupils, against the general background noise of the classroom?
50. Does he respond accurately to questions or directions?
51. Does his own speech suggest that he is hearing sounds accurately?
52. Can he differentiate between different speech sounds?

    three-tree   ball-bell   fall-wall   bed-pad

Motor Readiness

A certain measure of motor readiness is necessary if a pupil is to handle the tools of reading: books, papers, pencils etc. This is also important where writing and drawing are to be related to reading.

53. Can the pupil handle books reasonably well?
54. Does he form letters well when writing from copy?
55. Are the hand and eye well coordinated when using tools, sounding balls etc?
56. Can he do simple jigsaws successfully?

General Notes

The factors when considering reading readiness are many and varied. Ideally a teacher should work out her own observation schedule for such assessment. Careful analysis of these records will also indicate the most suitable approach to the learning task, phonic or whole word approach etc.

How to check whether the child is developing normally or not:

Vineland Social Maturity Scale
Age 0-1
1. Laughs
2. Balances head
3. Grasps objects within reach
4. Reaches for familiar persons
5. Rolls over
6. Reaches for nearby objects
7. Occupies self unattended
8. Sits unsupported
9. Pulls self upright
10. Imitates sounds
11. Drinks from the cup with assistance
12. Moves about on the floor
13. Grasps with thumb and finger
14. Demands personal attention
15. Stands alone
16. Follows simple instructions

Age 1-2
1. Walks about unattended
2. Marks with pencil
3. Masticates food
4. Transfers objects
5. Overcomes simple obstacles
6. Fetches or carries familiar objects
7. Drinks from cup unassisted
8. Plays with other children
9. Goes about the house

10. Discriminates edible substances
11. Walks upstairs unassisted
12. Talks in short sentences
13. Knows his pet name

Age 2-3
1. Asks to go to the toilet
2. Initiates own play activities
3. Removes dress
4. Gets drink unassisted
5. Dries own hands
6. Avoids simple hazards
7. Puts on dress unassisted
8. Relates experiences
9. Recognises familiar objects
10. Copies a circle
11. Defines simple object
12. Repeats three digits
13. Knows his correct name

Age 3-4
1. Walks down the steps
2. Plays co-operatively
3. Buttons dress
4. Helps in little household tasks
5. Performs for others
6. Washes hands unaided
7. Counts four coins
8. Names objects through memory
9. Differentiates lengths
10. Knows father's name
11. Knows parts of the body
12. Counts from 1-10

Age 4-5
1. Cares for self at toilet
2. Washes face unassisted
3. Goes about the neighbourhood unassisted
4. Dresses self except for tying
5. Uses pencil or crayon for drawing
6. Plays competitive exercise games
7. Repeats five digits
8. Recognises four coins
9. Copies a square
10. Knows left and right
11. Repeats small sentences
12. Counts 1-30

Age 5-6
1. Uses bicycle, play scooter etc
2. Prints simple word
3. Plays simple table games
4. Is trusted with money
5. Goes to school unattended
6. Names colours
7. Differentiates between simple objects
8. Recognises six coins
9. Comprehends
10. Differentiates similar objects

Age 6-7
1. Uses pencil for writing
2. Bathes unassisted
3. Goes shopping unassisted
4. Adds money
5. Counts 1-20
6. Names similarities

7. Counts three digits backwards
8. Counts five digits forward

Age 7-8
1. Reads time to the quarter hour
2. Uses knife for cutting
3. Participates in organised field games
4. Combs or brushes hair
5. Knows the days of the work
6. Knows dates
7. Can define dissimilarity

Age 8-9
1. Uses tools
2. Performs routine household tasks
3. Reads on own initiative
4. Bathes unaided
5. Recognises absurdity
6. Makes small purchases and brings correct change

Age 9-10
1. Cares for self at the table
2. Makes minor purchases
3. Goes around the locality freely
4. Repeats long sentences
5. Constructs sentences
6. Names the months
7. Repeats four digits backwards
8. Recognition of absurdities
9. Vocabulary approximately 40 words

With the help of these scales, parents can easily check whether their child is developing or not.

ooo

7

How to Treat Common Learning Difficulties

Common Learning Difficulties and Methods of Treatment

Symptoms	Useful Methods of Treatment
Mispronunciation and confusion of similar words and vowels	Speech training. Lists of similar words given (a) of similar consonants and vowels orally (b) visually. Practice in recognising letters heard and seen. Training in analysis of words.
Reversals	Emphasis on direction of reading by exercises involving tracing. Phonic analysis also helps.
Repetitions new words. slow rate. tape.	Training in methods of learning. Encouragement of calmness and Reading aloud with pupils and
Substitutions	Word games in which phonic analysis is emphasised. Use of easier material. Enlargement of vocabulary.
Additions or omissions	Emphasis on meaning. Flash cards with incomplete sentences and complete ones for comparison. Reading in concert with teacher.

Frequent pausing and hesitation	Enlargement of vocabulary. Practice with flash cards showing unfamiliar words. Use of easier material.
Omission of lines	Use wider spacing. Underline with card. Reduce anxiety.
Jerky reading, word by word	Reduction of emphasis on words. Training with sentence or phrase flash cards, to which responses are made.
Lack of intelligent interpretation	Use easier material. Emphasis on meaning. Provision of motive for reading. Practice with sentence flash cards.
Excessive vocalisation	Increased training in silent reading. Discourage lip movements. Practice with flash cards to enlarge sight vocabulary and to develop correct eye movements. (Bring card from behind screen from left to right.)
Difficulty in recalling	Practice in summarising easier material.
Inability to read quickly	Practice in skimming to locate words or phrases in paragraph or sentence or page, (a) orally, (b) in writing.
Difficulty in noting details	Use of completion exercises. in description Underlining correct answers. Construction of question on a given paragraph. Extension of spoken vocabulary to give greater security and familiarity with words.
Intellectual development; defiant behaviour; group or individual test results	Immaturity shown by marked delay in commencement of formal reading and concentration on

sound reading readiness scheme. Accent on visual and auditory discrimination, motor control, vocabulary and articulation. Real-life experiences are most valuable.

Visual Efficiency

Careful observation shows child frequently rearranging material on his desk, squinting and complaining of headaches.	Make classroom adjustments: consult specialist. Do not delay reading.

Visual Discrimination

Gross errors in matching work, etc.	Lots of practice with matching, sorting etc. No need to delay reading introduction as long as matching is carried out in parallel.

Auditory Efficiency

Observation shows inattention, misunderstanding of directions or continual requests to repeat instructions.	Refer to specialist (audiologist) and make classroom adjustments. Do not delay reading instruction.

Auditory Discrimination

Noticed mainly by poor sensitivity to sounds and poor habits of attending to similarities in word sounds. word channel sounds.	Undertake auditory training. Do not delay reading instruction but continue attending to similarities in parallel. Use stronger visual

General Physical Conditions

Noticed by teacher's observation, signs of fatigue, irritability, listlessness, paleness or excessive coloration.	Ensure medical attention, adjust methods to avoid fatigue and delay reading if necessary, or as advised by medical adviser.

Personal and Emotional Factors

Observation by teacher or through maturity tests. Signs are shyness, over-boisterousness, worry, fear, building withdrawal, daydreaming.	Seriously consider delaying reading instruction and concentrate on confidence-building measures.

ooo

8

Caring for Handicapped Children

Handicapped children are generally divided into the following categories:
1. Physically handicapped
2. Mentally handicapped
3. Blind
4. Deaf and dumb

Generally, in an attempt to make life easy for their handicapped child, parents are overly helpful. This is not good for the child. Instead, he should be expected to lead a life as nearly normal as possible within the limits of his handicap. Therefore, he should not be excused from his duties and responsibilities.

First, we will discuss the different types of handicap in children.

CRIPPLING AND HEALTH DISABILITIES

These children are generally categorised in the following main types:

Cerebral palsy: This is an impairment of the nervous system that cannot be considered a disease in the usual sense. Rather, the term designates numerous types of neuromuscular disabilities, which are characterised by disturbances of motor function resulting from damage to the brain and the central nervous system. Some of the symptoms of cerebral palsy include muscle weakness or flaccidity, excessive involuntary motion, postural imbalance, and spasticity.

The damage to the central nervous system, which causes cerebral palsy, may occur before birth, at the time of birth, or during the early years of life. Parental factors that may predispose the foetus to damage include: blood type incompatibility, especially the RH- factor, maternal infections (particularly Rubella) and occasionally other virus diseases, Toxemia, a condition associated with the presence of toxic substances in the mother's blood, conditions that cut off the supply of oxygen to the foetus' brain or affect the oxygen-carrying properties of the mother's blood, such as severe anaemia, prematurity, diabetes, and X-ray therapy.

During birth, the conditions that can cause brain damage are prolonged labour, difficult or abnormal birth, such as breech birth; the cord twisted around the throat; precipitant birth; excessive birth weight; and obstetrical procedures, such as forceps delivery. Factors that may be responsible for damage in the early years of life are infections of brain tissues, such as encephalitis; mechanical damage to the brain; poisons, such as lead poisoning, and progressive neurological disorders.

Most children with cerebral palsy have other multiple handicap conditions that complicate the educational problem. The most prevalent secondary handicaps in cerebral palsied children are speech impairment and mental retardation. Visual and auditory impairment is also common.

Epilepsy: Epilepsy is a sudden onset and sudden offset phenomena affecting consciousness and/or sensory motor or automatic functions.

Epileptic, or convulsive, seizures result from spontaneous, uncontrolled firing of neurons in the brain. Lesions which cause the seizure may be either organic or biochemical and may stem from some structural defect in the brain due to metabolic disorders, nutritional deficiencies, genetic factors, accidents, or prenatal or birth injury, or temporary conditions including digestive upsets, high temperature, or acute infection.

HEARING DISABILITIES

A defect in one or more parts of the ear and its associated nerve pathways leading from the ear to the brain prevents the child from adequately hearing, perceiving, or attending to either faint speech, ordinary conversational speech, or loud speech.

Those whose hearing loss is so severe at birth and in the prelingual period, considered before two to three years of age, that it precludes normal, spontaneous development of spoken language are called deaf.

Those whose hearing loss in the prelingual period or later is not of sufficient severity to preclude the development of some spoken language, and those who have normal hearing in the prelingual period but acquire hearing loss later, are called *partially hearing*.

An endogenous-type auditory defect is transmitted from parents to the child as an inherited trait. Exogenous defects result from disease, toxicity, accident, or injury, which inflicts damage on any part of the auditory system, thus affecting its capacity to receive and transmit sound. While auditory impairments – the result of damage to the auditory nerve pathways leading through the brain stem to the auditory area of the cortex of the brain – represent Central Auditory Dysfunction and may exist independent of any other problems.

A common obstruction in the outer ear is excessive secretion of earwax; another is insertion of objects such as beans, peas, and other foreign bodies into the canal by young children. The middle ear cavity into the back of the nose and throat is very readily subject to invasion by bacteria or viruses from the Eustachian tube. Almost every individual suffers ear infection at least one or more times in his life even though he or his parents may not be able to remember such an occurrence.

Another cause for the high prevalence of ear infections in young children is the tendency toward adenoids, which form a spongy mass around the nasopharyngeal opening of the Eustachian tube, sometimes completely obstructing it. Blockage of this tube creates a vacuum in the middle ear, which in turn prevents proper ventilation of the middle ear cavity. The secretion of fluid by the mucous membrane lining of the middle ear then cannot drain out normally and soon becomes a ready medium for the invasion of bacteria from the nasopharynx. An acute ear infection can then occur. Chronic or repeated infections are apt to form deposits of adhesive scar tissue on the eardrum itself and around the joints of the ossicular chain, making the sound transmission system much less flexible. This stiffening can depress hearing levels from a mild to moderate degree, depending upon the amount of such formation.

It is well established that maternal Rubella (German measles) can seriously affect not only the hearing of the unborn child but cardiac vision and mental functions as well. Rock and roll type music in public places and hazardous noise levels are also responsible for hearing loss.

The emphasis on early detection of hearing loss and the use of electronic hearing aids have made notable possible advances in the development of nursery and kindergarten programmes for hearing-impaired children.

VISUAL DISABILITIES

Children with visual disabilities are those who differ from the average to such a degree that special personnel, curriculum adaptation and/or additional instructional materials are needed to assist them in achieving at a level commensurate with their abilities.

It is misleading to think of children with visual disabilities as a separate group when their basic educational needs are generally similar to those of normal sighted children.

The visually impaired child lacks natural excitation from the visual sense. He is not stimulated by vision to traverse to the object. This stimulation could be provided from listening, feeling, tasting, and smelling. The implication points to the use of instructional methods that include stimulation through the use of the remaining sensory modalities.

MENTAL RETARDATION

This is a state of arrested or incomplete development of the mind, so severe that the patient is incapable of leading an independent life or of guarding himself against serious exploitation or, in the case of a child, being capable when he grows into an adult.

Mentally retarded children are classified according to their intellectual level. Those with an Intelligent Quotient below 25 are classified as *severe*. Those with an IQ of 25-50 are *moderate*. Those with an IQ of 50-75 are *mild*.

HANDICAPPED CHILDREN NEED SPECIAL EDUCATION

Now most teachers recognise that each child is different from the other. Furthermore, they are aware that every individual has a unique profile of characteristics. Consequently, educators are today making more provisions than ever before to individualise instructional programmes to fit the unique needs of each pupil.

Pupils with special abilities or unusual limitations are known as exceptional children. The programmes, procedures and devices, like those just cited, do not provide for the appropriate educational needs of such pupils. If these children are to be given as great an opportunity to reach their potential as normal children do, they require a programme of *special education*, ranging from a short period of time to many years.

As far as mentally retarded children are concerned, there is no single way to look after their social, physical and educational development. They are as different as any other group of people. As such, they need individually tailored programmes to facilitate development of their skills. Our society is gradually beginning to facilitate development of their skills and recognising that the mentally retarded deserve the best. For too long they have been viewed as sub-human, social non-contributors. It has taken a long time to reverse the tide of negativity against them.

Through theory, research, and practice, behavioural scientists have recognised that the basic principles of behaviour that have stood the test of all time with normal individuals are no different for the mentally challenged. Today, all levels of government have become more active in supporting research and training efforts for the mentally challenged.

ooo

Typical Adaptive Behaviour Expectancies

Intellectual Levels (Approximate IQ Scores)	Age Levels		
	Pre-school (under 6)	School Age (6-18)	Adult (over 18)
Mildly retarded (60 ± 5 to 75 ± 5)	Slightly slow in walking, talking, and caring for self; but usually indistinguishable from normal children and therefore unidentified before entering school.	Capable of learning academic skills between the 3rd and 6th-grade levels only; therefore literate.	Capable of vocational, personal, and marital independence; thus most lose identification in adulthood. The more retarded may need some supervision and guidance.
Moderately retarded (35 ± 5 to 60 ± 5)	Noticeably slow in learning self-help skills; but usually learn to walk, feed self, and speak simply; toilet training will be minimal at this age.	Capable of school learning between kindergarten through 3rd grade; therefore still typically illiterate.	Capable of employment in supervised unskilled occupations, often only in sheltered workshops; very rarely attempt marriage or unsupervised independent living.

Severely retarded (20 ± 5 to 35 ± 5)	By 6, may finally have learned to walk and feed self, but very little toileting, speaking, or other self-help skills at this age.	Capable only of rudimentary learning of non-academic skills in areas of self-care, and elementary speech.	Some capable of performing chores and other simple tasks even in home or sheltered workshop. Need permanent care from parents, relatives, or society.
Profoundly retarded (below 20 ± 5)	Usually learn at best minimal ambulatory skills; rarely any feeding, speaking, toileting, or other self-help skills; many permanently bed-bound.	Some capable of ambulation and feeding; many continue being permanently bed-bound and helpless.	Incapable of any self-maintenance or vocational usefulness; need permanent nursing care.

Source: Adapted from Sloan and Birch, 1955, p. 262.

www.ingramcontent.com/pod-product-compliance
Lightning Source LLC
Chambersburg PA
CBHW070336230426
43663CB00011B/2344